TEACHING CHARACTER THROUGH SPORT:
Developing a Positive Coaching Legacy

Bruce Eamon Brown

Throughout this book, the masculine shall be deemed to include the feminine and vice versa.

ISBN: 1-58518-729-1
Library of Congress Control Number: 2002112754
Cover design: Jennifer Bokelmann
Book design: Jeanne Hamilton

Coaches Choice
P.O. Box 1828
Monterey, CA 93942
www.coacheschoice.com

DEDICATION

To all the people who call coaching their profession.

We must use the gifts we have been given, because "leaders are judged not by the numbers that are led, but by the numbers served."

"We have gifts that differ according to the grace given to us: prophecy, in proportion to faith; ministry, in ministering; the teacher, in teaching."
— Romans 12:6-7

And so, we are drawn in by the call that we feel in our souls— the call to coaching.

ACKNOWLEDGMENTS

I would like to thank my friend and colleague, Dr. Jim Peterson, for his wisdom, perspective, energy, insight, and time with this project.

FOREWORD

I am honored to write this foreword for Bruce Brown's *Teaching Character Through Sport: Developing a Positive Coaching Legacy*. While I know that Bruce has written other works, I am caught by the tie between the Bruce Brown that I know and the title that he has selected. Because above all else that Bruce Brown is – a deeply committed husband and father, a friend to many – he is a coach. Even after all the years he spent as an active coach, today, each day he is still someone's mentor, someone else's confidant, and yet another person's motivator. Each day he is still a coach.

Yet Bruce Brown is more. He has the desire and the ability to teach others what it takes to be a good coach through his spoken and written words. Each person who hears or reads Bruce's insights for the first time soon realizes that Bruce is an extraordinary individual who has the uncanny ability always to see the bright side and to believe in the goodness within us all. Furthermore, he possesses the unique ability to teach each person how to unlock the potential in all of those with whom we come in contact.

Bruce Brown understands the importance of leaving a positive coaching legacy of teaching that will have a meaningful impact on many generations. He works tirelessly to communicate the value of each person's role, whether as a coach, official, parent, or administrator, in developing youth who grow into positive, contributing adults.

Bruce has written an exceptional book. Each chapter provides the insight and guidance necessary to improve every individual as a coach and as a human being. Tied together in one book, these chapters provide a powerful message, with easy-to-understand principles, that will be simple to incorporate every day as a coach, family person, and responsible citizen.

I know that this book will make a difference in your life, and that it will assist you in making a difference in the lives of others. My thanks to Bruce for finally putting into the written word what he has lived and spoken about for so many years.

Mike Colbrese
Executive Director
Washington Interscholastic Activities Association

PREFACE

The title of "coach" doesn't change who you are per se. Rather, being a "coach" involves what you, as an individual, bring to the job. If you are a person with strong convictions, a strong work ethic, a positive attitude, and the ability to exert effective leadership, then you are a prototype of what the coaching profession should be all about.

As such, this book was written to address several critical issues for those individuals who really care about not only their profession, but also about those young people who are in their charge. *Part I: Making a Difference* examines why individuals go into coaching and what characteristics successful coaches tend to exhibit. *Part II: Teaching Character Through Sport* reviews the values that sport should instill and offers suggestions on how coaches can effectively develop that value in their athletes. *Part III: Crafting a Team* details what qualities great teams frequently have and how coaches can make physically conditioning their teams a constructive part of the team-building process. Finally, *Part IV: Focusing on Other Issues* presents an overview of how coaches can help transition their athletes within the program and discusses the role parents should have in the athletic experience of their children.

Hopefully, this book will enable coaches to have a better appreciation for their rightful responsibility to instill positive value in their athletes. If, in the process of reading this book and considering the points that have been made in it, coaches gain a meaningful understanding of their solemn duty in this regard, then the book will have achieved its intended purpose.

B.B.

CONTENTS

PART I

Making a Difference

"A great man is made up of qualities that meet or make great occasions."

— James Russell Lowell

CHAPTER 1

The Heart of the Matter

So, you're a coach. What does that mean to you? Hopefully, that means that you understand how truly fortunate you are to be part of one of the greatest professions in the world. You care about young people. You treasure the opportunity to help mold young people's lives. In other words, because you live a life that reflects your convictions, you have chosen to be a "difference maker."

Being a Difference Maker

Coaches who are difference makers live purposeful lives. They are able to make a meaningful difference in the lives of others, in their schools, and in their communities because of who they are and what they do. Their ability to make a meaningful difference is a by-product of the fact that their professional lives embody certain qualities, including:

- They respect their sport, their staff, their players, their school's administrators, and themselves.

- They believe in themselves and in the basic goodness of others; they trust their own abilities.

- They live a principled life at all times.

- They show genuine concern for others.

- They accentuate the positive.

- They understand that they are responsible for their own attitude, actions, and habits.

- They have direction in their professional lives; they are in charge of their life.

- They are fully aware of their role and responsibilities as a coach, particularly as these duties relate to helping young people develop and inculcate positive values.

- They are able to prioritize what is important in their lives and in the lives of others; they are good time-managers.

- They are goal-oriented; they realize that a goal, without a date or timeline attached, is just a dream.

- They are good listeners; they seek and consider feedback from others.

- They exhibit poise under pressure.

- They love what they do.

Champions for Life

No one could reasonably argue that individuals get into coaching for money. While the compensation is certainly substantial for some high-profile coaches at the Division I level, the vast majority of coaches will never receive more than whatever the standard teacher's pay scale mandates in a particular school district. Even more telling, in this regard, is the fact that the number of coaches who volunteer their efforts to work with young people far exceeds the number of salaried coaches.

Rather, as the last point in the previous section stated, individuals coach because they love what they do. They love to coach, not because of how much money they make, but in spite of it. They love to coach, not because of their ability to lead their teams to victory, but because of their capacity to create an environment where their teams will play to the best of their God-given potential.

As a consequence, every coach who follows his heart, adheres to his convictions, and helps instill positive values and a sense of self-worth in young people is a difference maker . . . a successful difference maker in the game of life.

> *"A man will do only so much for a dollar, but he will die for a cause."*
>
> — Anonymous

CHAPTER 2

Common Traits Among Successful Coaches

> *"Coaching is not a natural way of life – your victories and losses are too clear cut; let's face it, we do not fit the profile of a mentally healthy person."*
>
> – Tommy Prothro

A number of successful methodologies are employed in the profession of coaching. Depending on the circumstances, some are more effective than others for a given situation. As such, each individual coach utilizes the strengths of his personality, as well as his experiences, to formulate his personal coaching style. On the other hand, several common threads can be seen in most successful coaches.

This chapter focuses on several of the most common traits among successful coaches. These traits not only contribute to individual success, but also to longevity in the profession. For discussion purposes, these traits are addressed within the context of the following focal areas:

- ❑ Philosophy
- ❑ Plan, organize, persist, learn, and adjust
- ❑ Teaching and simplifying the game
- ❑ Shared behavioral expectations
- ❑ Positive motivation

Philosophy

Good coaches are positive. Great coaches have a positive passion.
Good coaches have strong beliefs. Great coaches are believed.

Successful coaches have a philosophy that guides them and defines their teams. A disciplined coaching philosophy typically involves the following key factors:

- Successful coaches know who they are and they know what they really believe. They understand why they have chosen their particular profession.

- A strong coaching philosophy gives coaches something that can be relied on in any situation. It enables them to get through the inevitable tough times and great times with equal grace.

- Successful coaches do not imitate other coaches. They may look for qualities they want to model, but they find their own style, based upon their personality, and an appropriate balance of their strengths and weaknesses. Good coaches can be themselves and be happy. Even though you should continually work to improve your coaching skills and style, you must realize there are no perfect coaches. Most coaches who have any longevity in this profession have many times experienced a situation where they would like to "rewind the tape" of their behavior in a way that would enable them to change what they said or how they acted. This desire to change is often a result of the emotions inherent to the activity.

- Successful coaches have a philosophy that is specific to the sport they coach. Furthermore, coaches must isolate and develop specific philosophies for the different sections of the game they coach. For example, a football coach needs to develop specific belief attitudes about offense, defense, game coaching, practice coaching, participation, specialization, and squad selection, as well as coaching staff expectations.

A strong, well-thought-out philosophy gives coaches a chance to identify what things are truly essential to them and then eliminate all the time-consuming, non-essential factors. Among the common traits that frequently reflect the philosophies of successful coaches are the following:

- Successful coaches have a positive belief in themselves and the game they coach.

- Successful coaches are competitive, but also maintain a proper perspective. They always strive to win each game, but understand that if they have prepared well, losses are not failures and some teams and coaches can benefit from occasional defeats. A young coach I knew built a team of very talented, 12-year-old players and went through the season undefeated, winning over 40 games. While the success that this particular team experienced was certainly exceptional, it would have served both the team and the coach to have found an opponent who could have beaten them at least once. The lesson learned from a loss or two would have been that losing is not the end of the world; room for improvement always exists and there are always teams or individuals who are better.

- Successful coaches have a philosophy that promotes positive attitudes and positive behaviors. They look for the good in each athlete and are willing to confront behavior that is not acceptable in a manner that allows meaningful change to occur.

- Successful coaches are confident individuals who have the ability and skills to develop confidence in the people around them. Their confidence comes from a thorough knowledge of the techniques and fundamentals involved in their sport and from the ability to teach these techniques and fundamentals in such a way that they develop well-prepared, confident athletes. Confidence in athletes comes from being prepared. Such preparation promotes the feeling in individual athletes that they and their teammates will perform well. Athletic confidence is not overstated claims of an individual's ability or what someone believes the score will be. That approach is called anticipating the outcome. This kind of outspoken, bragging player can be compared to "barking dogs," or having "false confidence." The dogs that do the most barking (like poodles) are seldom the type of dog that is really dangerous. Beware of the dog that really knows it is tough and quietly growls, as opposed to the "yapper" who runs in circles, making lots of noise.

- Confident coaches and athletes avoid people who diminish the confidence of others. When the competition is over, confident coaches and athletes focus on their own performance and their own team without focusing on the skills or abilities of an opponent, or making an irrelevant comparison to a teammate. Confidence and poise are spread by example, especially when the example is modeled by leadership.

- Successful coaches know that preparing and providing small, steady successes, with appropriate positive reinforcement, spreads confidence. As such, successful coaches are aware that examples of true confidence should consistently be demonstrated and presented to their athletes. The coach trying to build true confidence in his players needs to arrange conditions to avoid confidence-cutting people. The profession of coaching constantly involves correction. The one instructional technique necessary to be able to correct and still build confidence in athletes is to criticize the act, not the person. It is much better to say, "use both hands," rather than, "you can't catch." It may involve a simple change in how the coach communicates, but it will make a dramatic difference to the athlete. The first statement sends the message that the athlete's technique needs improvement, and the individual is capable of making the correct change. The second statement tells the athlete that the individual is not very good.

Among the *challenging* issues that you can address that can assist you in the development of your personal coaching philosophy are the following:

- *Coaching as a profession—why are you doing this?*

- *The game you coach—why do you love this game?*

- *Your athletes—what are your expectations for them?*

- *Practice—if preparation is the key to true confidence, what do you want your practices to look like?*

- *The most important thing the athletes will get from this experience—what do you want the finished product to look like?*

- *The role character will play in your coaching—what life lessons can your sport teach and how are you going to teach them?*

> *"Coaching is fighting for the hearts and souls of men and getting them to believe in you."*
>
> — Eddie Robinson

Plan, Organize, Persist, Learn, and Adjust

Good coaches plan. Great coaches plan every detail.

Successful coaches are prepared and organized. Great coaches plan, persist, learn, and adjust. They set goals, keep looking for methods that will allow them to improve, and continue to visualize the finished product (the athlete). These coaches keep their eyes up and are not discouraged by small setbacks. They have the ability to teach athletes how to prepare. After individuals and teams have learned to prepare, they must take the next step and attribute all success to preparation.

> *"Develop a love of details, they usually accompany success."*
>
> — John Wooden

Plan and Organize

The fact that quality preparation provides confidence for coaches, athletes, and teams has already been discussed. The successful coach covers every detail. Developing the ability to combine the correct practice tempo and instill correct techniques requires careful planning and execution of the plan. Coaches should not confuse activity with achievement. Practices can be very active and energetic, yet achieve very little. The most important factors in effective practices and team improvement are:

- ❑ Focused attention of the athletes

- ❑ Focused effort of the athletes

- ❑ The coach's ability to teach the physical skills required

- ❑ The coach's use of practice time

With regard to organizing and conducting effective practices, the following points apply:

- It is extremely important how much knowledge you have, but far more important how much the players understand and can execute.

- Your success or failure as a coach will be in direct proportion to your ability to plan and teach.

- Factors you should consider to maximize the effectiveness of your team's practices and eliminate wasted practice time:

  ✓ How much time do you have in each practice, each week, each season

  ✓ How many players and assistant coaches do you have

  ✓ How much practice space do you have

- Each drill must have a specific purpose. Every minute of drill time needs to be directly applicable to your defensive or offensive system. Once learned, drills need to simulate game conditions as closely as possible.

- When teaching a drill, you should demonstrate the whole picture first. Explain the purpose and goal of the drill, as well as where it fits into the team system. Once introduced, break the drill down into teachable, achievable parts and begin slowly, adding difficulty and speed to work your way back to the complete skill. Drills are more efficient if the rotation of players is clearly defined.

- You need to assess the time spent and the effectiveness of every drill. The best method to do this is to keep a daily record of each practice with appropriate comments concerning the practice, while the practice is fresh in your mind.

- Practice preparation requires that you do the following:

  ✓ Write your plan. Develop a practice-plan form that will allow you to put your daily plan on paper.

  ✓ Post your plan. Once written, it will improve practice effectiveness to post your plan in a place where your team can read and study the plan before practice begins. This step provides a chance for additional learning to take place between practice sessions. Athletes with questions or learning problems have an opportunity to get help from the coach before they go to practice. Everyone gets a chance to think about the upcoming practice and anticipate what is going to be taught.

✓ Follow your plan. Coaches need to be flexible and make adjustments to their plan during practice, but generally, the closer you can follow your plan, the more productive your practice will be. If you consistently find yourself having to adjust practice to decrease or increase the amount you are teaching, you need to do a better job of pre-practice planning.

• Constantly look for small, additional time segments you can find to assist the learning of your athletes. Find pre-practice time in a space on the court or field that does not interfere with the team currently practicing. Use that time to meet, get your athletes' stretching done, cover the goals of practice, identify new skills or techniques, review previous practices, or give individual help. During practice, use "side practice" to pull out individual players who need individual attention, or to work on a specific skill that can be practiced in a small area. Assign assistant coaches a teaching responsibility in a side area and have them rotate each player through one at a time. Post-practice time can be used for any number of beneficial purposes, including to assess improvement or goals for the practice just concluded, give a heads up for the next practice, hand out any written material for learning or for parents, etc. Athletic homework is another method to obtain additional time. Athletes can have written or physical skill tests that can be completed at home, the results of which can be discussed at the next pre-practice.

• When planning your practice sessions, it is beneficial to vary the drills. Once a skill or drill has been introduced and taught, shorten the duration of the drill and get the same number of repetitions without requiring the same amount of time. Repetition is the key to motor learning. Improvement will come naturally if you give your athletes small doses of the skill, repeated regularly, at game speed and requiring maximum effort. Drills that go on too long often turn into unfocused activity that does not achieve the immediate goal. Drills done too casually tend to develop more bad habits than good.

Vary your drills by performing physically demanding drills, followed by one that is physically easier. This coordinated scheduling of drills not only enables you to achieve your conditioning goals for your team, but also to create an optimum learning environment for your players.

New drills and complex concepts should be scheduled for early in practice, when players' minds are fresh and energy is high. Drills designated for the end of practice should be simple, but involve fundamentals that need to be executed successfully when players are tired.

If the players have met your expectations for a productive practice, then the last drill of the day should be fun. Coaches should try to end practice on a positive note — one that leaves the players smiling and looking forward to coming back.

- By naming your drills, you can avoid having to describe the drill each time you want to change drills. One of the best methods of naming drills is to use players' names. Identify the best player to have ever done the drill, and give it his or her name (e.g., the Miller drill). This step will accomplish several goals. First, it identifies the drill without description, and second, it provides motivation for players to either do the drill better than the person it is named after or to get a different one named after them. It also gives your program some sense of history, with drills named after players from your past teams or seasons.

- In order to increase individual improvement and team motivation, make every drill as competitive as possible. Usually, this step involves nothing more than finding a way to keep score or compete together against the clock.

- As much as possible, get team conditioning done during the drill section of practice. Drills should be done at game speed, lines should be short, and drill planning should be done with conditioning in mind. By not having to schedule time specifically for running, the coach has more teaching time and still gets the conditioning required for success.

- To increase the number of repetitions each player gets, teach and demonstrate to the whole group and then break into smaller groups. Drills done in small groups ensure accountability and increase opportunities for attempts, correction, and improvement.

- One of the keys to learning is for the coach to teach the skill correctly the first time. Players will learn the most from the first demonstration of any skill. Skills that are not taught correctly the first time require a lot of time to reverse the learning that has taken place.

- Attentiveness is one of the most important requirements of a good learning environment. You need to learn how to *get* and *hold* the focus of the athletes you are trying to coach. Attentiveness is a choice, and players can be held accountable for their focus. You need to do everything you can in the practice area to avoid distractions. If it requires removing extra people or dismissing inattentive players from practice to eliminate distractions and improve learning, it is worth it. You need to have an "attention-getter" (whistle or voice command) that allows the players to immediately stop all activity and focus on the coach. One area that will help attentiveness that you have control over is how long you speak. You should try to keep verbal instruction periods short. Use concise terminology and descriptions and spend more time on the physical repetitions. *Say it once, say it right, and require your players' full attention.* If you find yourself repeating the same instructions, your athletes are getting the message that it is not required to listen the first time, because if they wait, it will be repeated.

- In your attempt to cover every detail, do not overlook any items that will benefit from rehearsal. For example, practice what you want your team to do during a timeout, halftime, when substituting, etc.

- Teach to the level of your fastest learners. Be willing to stay and help the slower learners catch up no matter how long it takes, but during practice, move at a pace of your quickest learners. This method helps your more advanced players stay focused and motivated, and still provides dignity for the players who require more help. Most behavioral problems in practice occur during periods of boredom. Keep players moving, motivated, and focused.

- If you find that one player is not getting a particular concept or skill that the rest of the team has learned, do not stop the whole team to work with the individual. Have that player move to the side to work with an assistant for correction without stopping the progress of practice.

- To assist cutting down on the transition time between drills, you or one of your managers can call out the name of the next drill that your players will do, with about 30 seconds to a minute left in the one they are doing. Players will learn to listen like it is a 30-second warning and be ready to move right into the next drill on the whistle.

- In order to plan your whole season, you need to develop a master checklist with everything that needs to be taught. Put everything in writing on a season-long calendar. Once you have established the complete list, it will allow you to prioritize the things that are truly essentials and separate them from the non-essentials that you may not get to during the season. A master checklist will also provide a starting point for coaches to divide up responsibilities.

Persist

> *"If you are plowing a field and you come to a stump, you don't stop plowing, you just plow around it."*
>
> — Unknown

The ability to stay the course, to not be discouraged, to continue to battle regardless of any obstacles is what allows coaches to have longevity. You can always identify people who will eventually be successful because they have the inner strength to persevere. In coaching, you must continue to see the big picture and visualize the finished product. Temporary failures cannot blind you to your goals. There is only one guarantee in any athletic season; it will not be perfect. Problems will always occur with relationships, losses, injuries, and other challenges—some in your control and others that are out of your control.

Successful coaches have and model persistence. Stay with, and believe in, your kids. They need you, your persistence, and your faith in them much more than they are willing to admit. If you want to have teams that never quit, then you as a coach must have that same spirit. The time when the most positive persistence is needed is when things are not going well. All cues for how the team will respond are taken from leadership. Develop the capacity to never quit. Be determined toward every goal. Continue to visualize the finished product. Do not let your team lose sight of their potential greatness. Great coaches do not coach against their opponent; they coach against a vision of how good their team is capable of being and never let go of that vision.

Continue to Learn and Adjust

> *"The height of insanity is doing the same thing over and over and expecting a different result."*
>
> – Albert Einstein

It is essential for both athletes and coaches to have a teachable spirit. Successful coaches never stop learning and improving by questioning and assessing their methods. The best coaches are on a constant search for better ways to teach the same skills, new or different techniques and strategies. One of the worst things that coaches do is to become defensive and protective of what they already know and are doing.

In order to continue improving, you need to consider the following steps:

*   One of the best methods for improving your ability to prepare is to go watch effective coaches conduct practices and teach. Identify the strongest coaches in your area, and go see them in action. Ask to see their plans, and even sit in on a planning session. In most cases, it really doesn't even make any difference if they are coaching the same sport. If you are looking at the ability to prepare, it may be both helpful and interesting to observe a different sport and see what common strategies are used. Effective practice coaches will demonstrate the same skills regardless of sport, age, or gender of the athletes involved.

*   Another helpful method to assess your own team and coaching style is to bring in trusted, experienced coaches from the outside to "scout" or evaluate you, your staff, and your team. This form of self-assessment may be the quickest method to improve your planning.

- Finally, it is essential that you constantly stretch your mind, stay current, and increase your knowledge base. The best ways to accomplish this are to attend coaching clinics, read coaching books, and watch coaching videos. Listen to every coach that you can possibly hear. It gives you an opportunity to enhance your knowledge of the technical aspects of your sport and to make a comparative analysis of your coaching methods.

Among the *challenging* steps that you can undertake with regard to being prepared and well-organized are the following:

- *Develop a written master checklist (skills, drills, offenses, defenses, situations, calendar).*

- *Prioritize everything on your list into categories of essentials and non-essentials.*

- *Identify and contact any coaches you would like to observe.*

- *Make a list of all coaching responsibilities and delegate within your staff and parents.*

Teaching and Simplifying the Game

Good coaches understand the game. Great coaches understand the game and their athletes and how to teach both. Good coaches understand the progression necessary to teach a physical skill. Great coaches can teach the physical skill, correct it, and persist to see that it is performed correctly during practice and games.

Teaching is the key to skill improvement, and skill improvement is the key to team improvement. Your job as a coach is to maximize the possibilities for learning by being the best teacher possible.

Teaching the Game

Understanding the *rules of motor learning* allows you to successfully teach a physical skill. The following four steps are involved in effectively teaching a particular physical skill:

❑ *Defining* is clarifying the skill, for example:

- Give an exact verbal blueprint of the skill.

- Introduce the terminology that will trigger the physical movement.

- Teach where this skill fits into the bigger picture.

❑ *Modeling* is learning by example and demonstration. Among the factors that can make modeling effective are the following:

- The effectiveness of modeling depends on how well the coach can get and hold the attention of the athletes. Effective coaches demand attention without any exceptions.

- Successful teachers talk less and show more. Coaches need to be able to demonstrate correctly or provide a model who can. Coaches cannot stop with a verbal description. After correctly demonstrating the skill, begin repetitions and corrections.

- To simplify learning, teach it right *the first time*.

- Because most coaches are trained to identify mistakes and correct them, many coaches need to learn to demonstrate the right way to do things. Do not spend time showing how it can be done incorrectly. Demonstrating the right way covers all the phases of learning athletes need to see.

❑ *Shaping* is guiding, continuing to mold a behavior or a skill. It may be the most important part of the whole skill-learning process. The coach must break a skill down into pieces. The more complex the skill, the more important shaping becomes. Shaping requires the following:

- An exact blueprint of how you will take an athlete from a beginning level of skill to as far as he is capable of progressing. This step requires planning.

- The coach must consistently identify and support any action that comes closer to the desired product and give direct and immediate correction when it is needed.

- Patience is required to shape correctly and the ability to positively persist is what allows better coaches to excel.

❑ *Reinforcement* involves communication between the coach and player that promotes learning. The best form of reinforcement is positive. One of the most effective forms of positive reinforcement is with your voice (praise and approval). Being "positive" doesn't mean you cannot be demanding, in fact the exact opposite is true. Being positive allows your athletes to take your efforts to correct them as a compliment and takes the fear out of failing for most athletes. Positive, demanding coaches understand how to combine teaching and correcting technique with a portion of empathy and caring. The principles of sound reinforcement include:

- The closer in time you give the reinforcement, the stronger the learning effect. Do not wait to verbalize either your praise or correction.

- Reinforce effort and behavior. Athlete-owned behaviors will allow skill improvement. Remember that you get whatever you reward. By rewarding effort and behavior, you get those qualities, and with effort and behavior, you will get a natural skill progression. By responding only to outcome or performance, you are limiting yourself and your athletes.

In summary, first you define, then you model, and finally you immediately begin shaping and offering positive reinforcement for any behavior that comes closer to the finished product. Your efforts at reinforcement do not have to wait for the athlete to perform the skill exactly.

> *"The eight laws of learning are explanation, demonstration, imitation, repetition, repetition, repetition, repetition, repetition."*
>
> – John Wooden

Simplifying the Game

Great coaches have the ability to make the game seem easy to learn and play. To put coaching in its simplest terms, look at what occurs frequently in the game and at the level you coach and get proficient at those things. Among the factors that hurt natural motivation and love of the game are the following:

- Defeats
- Negative coaching
- Mental or physical tiredness
- Making the game too complex

Understanding the Coach's Role During the Game—Game Coaching

You should incorporate the following general principles into your coaching style:

- Identify and use only behaviors that will help your team's performance.

- Model behavior that provides confidence, concentration, and poise. This step is the single most important contribution that you can make.

- Respond to adversity the way you want your athletes to respond. They will model what you do.

- Remember positive reinforcement. You must be the same person in a game as you are in practice.

- Focus on the performance of your team, and attempt to keep your attention off things you do not have any control over (e.g., the opponents, referees, the conditions, etc.).

- Keep the athletes as the main focus of the game. For whatever reason, some coaches feel the need to be the center of attention. They accomplish this by being very overactive, yelling, or trying to make every strategic decision for the team.

- Work hard for your team; each game is a puzzle waiting to be solved.

- Be careful with your words when things get emotional. Comments like, "I've taught you that," probably should be, "I need to teach that better." Comments like, "you guys can't hold a lead," "don't panic in the clutch," or "quit freezing up," often turn out to be prophetic.

- If you can't end the game on a positive note, say nothing at all and wait until the next practice. Most observations during the game are not as accurate as the ones you will have after you have analyzed the game tape. Avoid long post-game evaluations. What most kids need at this time is a quick, positive summary and an approach where you give them time and space. The corrections that you try to teach after a game will be better addressed in the following practice, when you can do something to correct them.

Shared Behavioral Expectations

Good coaches talk about their expectations. Great coaches have athletes that meet their expectations, because these coaches are strong enough to confront incorrect behavior and half-efforts and therefore get the love and respect of their athletes.

Great coaches understand that discipline is involved in all successes.

- Athletes must be taught that discipline is not a dirty word, but rather a positive statement that players can focus their attention and put the needs of the team ahead of their own. For the coach, it is the delicate balancing act of control with fun. A situation involving all discipline is more like forced labor, and all fun has no meaning or direction and usually results in wasted time and lack of improvement. These two need to be balanced, otherwise each may lose its effectiveness.

- As a coach, whatever behavior, effort, and attention you tolerate will be perpetuated year after year. If you do not correct a poor effort or behavior by calling it what it is, you are sending a message of acceptance.

- If a player enters your program with unacceptable behaviors, that is someone else's fault. If they represent and leave your program with the same unacceptable behaviors, that is entirely your fault. When attitudes require change, it is the coach's responsibility to change them.

> *"The only known substance from which a successful adult can be made is a child."*
>
> – Tom Lickona, *Raising Good Children*

You need to create a climate where positive changes can occur. When behavioral changes are going to be required, it is essential that you are willing to confront the behavior and understand how to create that change with a player. When mistakes of behavior are made, an opportunity for behavior change exists because behavior is an athlete-owned choice. The following steps can be used to allow the change to happen:

❑ Changing attitudes:

- Establish which behavioral choices are acceptable and which ones are not with every athlete, before any poor choices can occur.

- Look for the good in every athlete. More than anything else, players want your attention. You can choose how much time you give the player misbehaving, in comparison to the ones who are on track with full effort.

- Work year-round to make changes. Do not wait until the season begins (or for the first game or the first mistake), because you will be catching players doing things wrong, instead of being proactive.

- When a problem does occur, confront it quickly in an appropriate manner. Try not to embarrass the player, but do not allow the behavior to continue or escalate. Remain calm, call it what it is, for example: "your reaction to the umpire was not acceptable," "you need to be listening during instruction." Don't lose your temper, but rather think about the kind of confrontation you have with a policeman when you have made a mistake. If they stop you for going too fast, they don't come up to your car and scream at you about slowing down. They simply and calmly state what it was that you did and what the result will be. With regard to responding to a player who has exhibited an inappropriate attitude, confront what is wrong, and then immediately turn all your attention back to praising the players who are making correct choices and behaving appropriately.

- Have your responses to situations well-thought-out ahead of time, for example:

  ✓ "This is your chance to work on and demonstrate your poise, or you can sit down. Your choice."

  ✓ "We've talked about this situation and practiced what the correct response is."

  ✓ "That is not acceptable on this team, do not let your teammates down."

- When trying to change an athlete's behavior, talk and listen to him away from practice or a game. Eliminate the emotions of those situations, and allow both of you to get a different perspective. Look for the key that sets him off. Often, it could be an outside source (girlfriend/boyfriend, parents, or school). I have had college players living off campus who had poor effort in practice due to a poor diet. Other younger players, who because of their size had people place high expectations on their performance, knew they were not talented enough to live up to those unrealistic expectations, and developed a fear of failing in public. As a result, every mistake they made had to be someone else's fault (especially the referees').

- Be the one situation in their lives where they know the exact expectations, can count on consistency, and can feel good about themselves. They need to know you are their ally, as long as you are getting their best effort and behavior.

- Provide opportunities for the athlete to see the behavior as you see it. I have brought in a player to watch the game videotape of an unacceptable reaction to a teammate or official with just the two of us. Away from the crowd and the emotion, they normally see the behavior in the same light as the coach and are embarrassed and able to make the appropriate changes.

- If a player admits that they do not want to behave incorrectly and would like to change the behavior, you can ask if they want your help. In cases like this, I have used cues or keys to let the player know that you can see a certain behavior about to be tested or starting, but not to the point where it is a problem. For example, if you are attempting to stop a player from pouting when things go wrong and recover to get on with the next play, you may simply give that player a verbal cue. I call these "mood breakers," and often just use a nickname to let them know I can see a behavior beginning that they have said they want to change. At that point, they have a quick decision to make. They can continue to pout and be removed from the game, or they can adjust their attitude and remain in the game. Since this involves a choice, there needs to be a limit to the number of warnings to make sure that they have truly changed, and you are not enabling the behavior to remain. Be on their side as long as they are sincerely trying to change, but be persistent that they make the changes necessary to be a good teammate.

- Be a model of the behavior you are asking them to exemplify. If they respect you as a coach, the players will be more likely to take on your characteristics.

> *"Young people need models, not critics."*
>
> – John Wooden

- At some point, the coach needs to ask whether it is actually possible to change the inappropriate behavior of a specific player. On rare occasions, it may not be. Fortunately, the profession of coaching allows you to choose whom you work with and whom you choose to not work with. If you have made every attempt to make positive behavioral changes during the off-season, and your efforts have not worked, it is wise to use the date of squad selection as the dividing line. One hard day of cutting people with good talent but bad attitudes is better than three or four miserable months. Regardless of a player's ability, bad attitudes are team killers. Teams made up of people with great character do not deserve to have the coach sacrifice their season for a player with ability, but no character.

Talk about your expectations before the tryouts begin, and if you have been working with players year-round, it will be difficult to be fooled. In this regard, I have used the following definition for an appropriate athletic attitude: *Be aggressive, confident, disciplined and love to compete. Be intelligent enough to listen and develop the ability to work and to learn. Have faith in the people you are working with and always put the team ahead of yourself. Keep your sense of humor. Do not let your teammates down in anything you do.*

- Coaches successful at changing attitudes have a style that encourages and allows young people to change. Your main objective should be to use athletics to build positive attitudes and provide positive experiences.

- Occasionally, you may have to acknowledge when you may have been wrong in your assessment and, even more importantly, when actual positive changes have been made, give the athlete ownership of the new behavior ("look who you have become"). Acknowledgment may only take a private wink or a smile or possibly public recognition with spotlighting or a letter home.

With regard to establishing an environment where positive player behavior is the norm, you should address the following *challenges:*

- *Do a style check to see if you have encouraged a climate where change can occur.*
- *Write a profile of what you want an athlete in your program to look like. Include both behavior and work habits.*
- *Write and post your definition of a great athletic attitude.*
- *Identify and be willing to work with potential players year-round to ensure character development.*
- *Identify and use positive character traits as part of your squad selection process.*
- *Work with your entire coaching staff to see if you can agree on shared expectations for athletic behavior.*
- *If you are not supported by your administration when it comes to confronting and changing bad attitudes, you are coaching in the wrong place.*

Positive Motivation

Good coaches encourage and motivate. Great coaches motivate through love and get every ounce of attention and energy from their athletes. They can get people to do all that they are capable of and enjoy it.

Great coaches can take a negative and turn it into a positive. Motivation is simply the force that propels a person or group into action. As a coach, you must decide what is important to you and then attempt to find ways to make those things important to your athletes. A motivated team requires a common agreement between all the participants concerning high expectations for the team. A motivated team exhibits a high desire to succeed by everyone involved.

Eight Keys for Individual and Team Motivation:

#1. *Communicate*. The greatest motivational principle in coaching is that *things that get rewarded, get done, and they will perpetuate themselves.* Some qualities that a coach will communicate quickly to a new group of athletes include knowledge, honesty, consistency, sincerity, and level of preparation. When athletes are assured that you possess these qualities, they will be more likely to accept you. With this acceptance, learning comes easier. The coach should be comfortable being direct with both correction and praise. Coaches who communicate well develop a level of trust with their athletes. This trust allows them to dignify honest mistakes by sending the message, "mistakes are part of learning and as long as you are giving your complete attention and full effort, you will improve."

#2. *Build on successes*. Coaches who can motivate can identify and build on successes. Small successes lead to bigger successes. It doesn't take much to let an individual athlete know you have seen him improve. It is said that most people can live on a compliment for a month. If that is true, imagine what it would mean to an athlete to get at least one compliment a day (if it is deserved). Catch people doing things better and give direct praise. *When verbalizing praise, use the athlete's name and the action she did.* "Good job" is praising, but "good job, Sarah, for using the correct hand" is a much more effective message to Sarah and also to her teammates.

#3. *Be consistent and persistent*. People who can motivate are consistent and persistent. Be the same positive demanding coach every day. Do not let the inevitable small bumps in the road discourage you.

#4. *Be creative*. Creative coaches who obviously enjoy their work are able to bring a joy to practice every day and have a distinct advantage when it comes to motivating. They look for the keys that motivate different players. It may be as simple as using the players' nicknames or as complex as understanding problems in the athletes' lives outside of the team. Search for creative ways to begin or end practice or to teach specific skills. Turn the routine into the unusual. If you love the game, the athletes, and the team, then let your attitudes show.

#5. *Be positive*. Just like it is for athletes, your daily attitude is a choice. "Choices are the hinges of destiny." Be positive about yourself, other people, and life in general. Positive coaching input turns into positive team output.

#6. *Find value*. Coaches, who can motivate, teach, find and model individual worth attempt to find the good in every athlete with whom they have chosen to work. Motivational leadership shows genuine care, respect, and love. One of the best methods for being creative, positive, and able to demonstrate value in someone or some particular act is by doing post-game "spotlighting" (refer to Part II, "Teaching Character Through Sport").

#7. *Do the extra things*. Build up your team and show them value by working on methods that honor them. Coaches can use weekly newsletters, highlight videos, scrapbooks, and/or letters to parents. While these all take some extra time and effort, making the extra effort may be as simple as using humor, remembering birthdays, or being willing to spend time rebounding for a player who wants to shoot after practice.

#8. *Model motivation*. Just like any other skill that you are trying to teach, the coach needs to be a model of motivation. Each coach must decide what is important to him and then model it. All factors being equal, your athletes will take on your characteristics. If you expect your teams to be motivated, bring your love and enthusiasm to work daily, be demanding of yourself, and require your own personal best at all times.

Among the *challenging* activities that may assist you in motivating your team are the following:

- *Meet with your coaches and identify ways you can improve your communication efforts to your players, to staff, to parents, and to the community.*

- *Be willing to do some self-assessment. Listen to former athletes on ways you could have communicated better. Listen to hear what their memories are. Keep in mind that what they remember will often be the extremes (i.e., the most positive or most negative experiences).*

- *Challenge your creativity, for example, look for different methods to teach the same skills, for fun ways to end practice, and for opportunities to build relationships and teams.*

- *Examine ways you and your staff can go the extra mile for individual players and your teams. Be willing to do the small things that will build lifetime friendships and memories.*

PART II

Teaching Character Through Sport

"Our world is a college, events are teachers, happiness is the graduation point, character is the diploma God gives man."

— **Newell Dwight Hillis**

CHAPTER 3

More Than X's and O's

Sow a thought, reap an act.
Sow an act, reap a habit.
Sow a habit, reap a character.
Sow a character, reap a destiny.

— Author Unknown

The state of affairs in sport in our society is often reflected in the daily reports and newspaper articles that appear nationwide. The headlines and media are filled with accounts of irresponsibility, greed, selfishness, and corruption. Unfortunately, this ongoing stream of information reflects not only what is happening, but what is accepted as part of the inherent culture of sport. Every day something can be found about:

- Player probations
- Suspensions
- Arrests
- Steroid or other drug use
- Physical violence in games

- Spousal abuse
- Confrontations with officials
- Hiding or ignoring rules violations
- Fan violence
- Coaches kicked out of games

At times, the damning news concerning sports seems to be endless. The following recent events reflect the despondent state to which sport has sunk:

- An NBA owner jumping and waving his arms under the basket to distract a free throw shooter
- A "professional" football player stealing from a teammate's locker
- Fans throwing beer bottles on the field, at the referees, and at opposing players to protest a call

- A college player having to be restrained from going after an official and then spitting on a cheerleader when he has to be physically removed from the floor
- The "All-Pro" NFL wide receiver saying he will only play hard when he feels like it— weeks later, his *coach* gets fired
- The colleges and high schools that build winning teams "by hook or by crook"
- Universities that have a zero percent graduation rate in some athletic teams

Even the younger participants in sport have not been immune to the onslaught of questionable behavior. Among the specific examples of such conduct at the youth-sport level are the following:

- Required "Silent Sundays" on youth soccer fields
- A star Little League player whose father lied about his age, discovered to be two years older than the 12-year-old limit
- A youth baseball umpire whose tires are slashed
- A 15-year-old soccer referee being punched by a parent after a game for 10-year-olds
- A high school football coach spraying a slippery substance on the uniforms of his players to make them harder to tackle
- The constant transferring of students to high schools to be in an elite program
- The Little League hockey dads who got into a fight at practice – one of whom died during the fracas

A Time for Change

Sport, by its nature, is an activity that provides an intense form of public scrutiny, as well as individual self-evaluation. As too often has been seen at every level, rules are ignored, values give way to expediency, and models of character in sport become harder and harder to find. Does the culture of sport need to change?

All factors considered, everyone can probably agree that at some level changes are clearly needed in the world of sport. Most coaches can excuse themselves by saying "my players would never be involved in those type of things, and we can't really do anything about those situations." But there are some trickle-down effects that have become accepted behavior at many levels of sport that you may be able to relate to, for example:

- The player who believes it is alright to be late to practice or a meeting
- The player who looks away when being coached, ignoring you, or saying with his body language, "don't coach me"
- The player who points or signals "look at me" after a good play to draw attention
- The player who stares down the official after a judgment call

- The verbal taunting that has become commonplace in some sports after a rough play
- The pout or "attitude" displayed when a player is taken out of the game
- The foul language that has become acceptable within games and practices

On one hand, these are all small, subtle changes when compared to the other examples previously cited. On the other hand, they are significant and worth changing if we care about the real value of the sport experience. In a culture that is influenced so much by its sports teams and "stars," we must accept that many young people in our country will form their views of right and wrong from their observations and personal experiences in sport.

Research done by Anderson, Brewer, Van-Raalte and David (1996); Beller, Stoll, Burwell, Cole, and Hacker (1992 and 1996); Bredemeier, Weiss, Shields, and Shewchuck (1986) indicate the following:

- No documented support exists for the theory that participation in sport contributes to moral or character development. They found that participation actually inhibited character.
- The longer that athletes participated in sport, the greater negative disparity between them and their non-athlete peers.
- Women athletes tended to score higher in moral reasoning than men athletes.
- Athletes who participate in individual sports score higher in moral reasoning than those in team sports (just the opposite of what most individuals who coach team sports would have believed).

It is time that coaches (and parents) work together to raise young people who realize that sport is only a part of life, and being athletic does not serve as a guarantee of special privileges. Athletes must be taught and remember that they are no better than anyone else, and should act accordingly. Look closely, and you will see people in many family homes who place an overemphasis on sports at the expense of sportsmanship. Unfortunately, the accepted path toward becoming an "athlete" for far too many young people in our society has often involved the following four stages:

❏ Stage # 1. Very early in their lives, we identify and begin to develop their abilities (doesn't sound wrong so far).

❏ Stage # 2. We focus on and allow them to focus on personal achievement (still acceptable).

❏ Stage # 3. They gain attention and applause – and in the worst cases, a sense of entitlement (i.e., "normal rules do not apply to me").

❏ Stage # 4. They begin to measure their success by the amount of abundance in their life (money, attention, possessions).

Something has gone wrong with that accepted path—can you find it? Character development is missing. The physical skills are intentionally trained, and the achievements rewarded, while the character development is merely presumed.

Too often with young athletes, there is a belief that the only thing needed for future success is athletic talent. While God-given skills are certainly important for success, they cannot guarantee happiness or a satisfying life. Who they truly are and what they have become are much more important than who they appear to be; in other words, their character. In our society, it has become easier and often more productive to be able to write a good resume, than it is to build a life based on character.

Developing and demonstrating character as an athlete means deciding to live by a series of difficult choices, based on principles and values that give your life deeper meaning. What begins with the effort to make a tough choice and then follow through with that choice, can eventually become habit in the life of a young person.

> *"Excellence is a habit. Ethical excellence comes as a result of habit. We are what we repeatedly do."*
>
> – Aristotle

Yes, the culture of sport needs to be changed. Yes, the profession of coaching has had a hand in creating the current conditions, but also, no one can have a larger positive influence in changing the culture of sport and the character of athletes than coaches. It is time for the coaching profession to refocus, self-evaluate, and take a stand. Coaching is doing, taking action, making a difference. A clear distinction exists between complaining and doing. When it comes to changing the culture of sport, members of the coaching profession need to stop focusing on the negative; coaches need to teach and promote the positive. As such, coaches can be the best promoters and catalysts for positive change.

Coaching and Leadership

The opportunity to work side-by-side with highly motivated athletes and coaches in an atmosphere of mutual respect, trust, and dependence is unique and priceless. The strength, energy, and lifeblood of the team flows through the coach. Just like parenting, no individual will completely understand the relationships and emotions involved in coaching until that person becomes a coach.

The primary role of coaches is to build lifetime character traits in the young people who are in their care. Helping young men and women understand the difference between right and wrong behavior and teaching them to have the courage to live by those standards makes the act of coaching an expression of love.

> *"A leader is a person who has the ability to get other people to do what they don't want to do and LIKE it."*
>
> – Harry Truman

To take former president Truman's quote a little further, coaches need to develop the ability to get players to not only "like it," but to have it become "who they are." In terms of personal growth, the biggest step is when athletes move from doing the right thing simply because they were told to do so, to living the correct behavior because they *choose* to do it. This is the step that signifies that it has become their personal character.

This book is designed for coaches because I believe that coaches are the key to creating change within the arena of sport. Changes are made one player at a time, one team at a time, one school at a time. It is true that character is best learned at home. Outside the home, coaches are often the only connecting link between values and the athlete. As well-meaning as most administrators are, the further removed people are from the student-athlete, the less chance they have for positive impact.

Ethical athletic leaders are able to instill respect and responsibility in their individual athletes and teams by providing a model and inspiring those around them to reach higher than they thought possible. Coaching is one of the few professions where leadership is immediately expected, appointed with the job, and accepted. It is not realistic or fair to assume positions of leadership without taking the responsibility—to all those you directly influence—of placing character at the heart of your leadership model.

As a coach, you get to choose your leadership style, but also the people with whom you choose to work. Unlike the normal classroom teacher, most scholastic and college coaches get to say, "I choose to work with that person and choose to not select that person." Using squad-selection criteria that involve character provides a simple method for establishing what is important to you as a leader. Coaches should keep in mind that all other factors being equal, athletes will rise to whatever standards you set for them. By letting them know ahead of time that your expectations for specific behavioral choices are essential and irrevocable, the standard has been set for the season. As such, character is a matter of choice for both the athlete and the coach. In that regard, an important issue must be addressed: does your leadership cultivate a spirit of honesty, respect, sportsmanship, integrity, and responsibility to all those in your care?

Coaching is a relationship-based profession. It is a relationship based on mutual trust, obligation, commitment, emotion, and shared vision of what is correct and good. By the nature of the job and being part of a team, coaching carries with it the charge of helping each other constantly work to make positive changes, while sharing common goals and values. In order to establish a sport environment where positive virtues are instilled, every coaching philosophy must begin with an ethical base that inspires others to build excellence in their lives, as well as on the field.

Do you believe that athletics should *teach* character? If so, then you, as a coach and leader, must *teach* it!

> *"To believe something and not live it is dishonest."*
> – Ghandi
>
> *"We acquire virtues by first exercising them. Whatever we learn to do, we learn by actually doing it: for example, we become builders by building, and harp players by playing the harp. In the same way, we become just (fair) by doing just (fair) acts, self-controlled by doing self-controlled acts, brave by doing brave acts."*
> – Aristotle

Aristotle would have been a good coach. What his quote is saying is that ethical excellence, just like athletic excellence, depends mainly on developing good work habits. In other words, if you want to develop good habits of ethical character (virtues), such as honesty and responsibility, then you need to actually practice being honest and responsible.

Occasionally a school administrator would question the right of a coach to "teach values in a public school." Such an attitude should make you want to double your efforts. If the purpose and cause of what you are doing is significant, the consequences are irrelevant. As a point of fact, the consequences of not using sport to teach and demand correct behavior far outweigh the concerns of cowardly, weak people whose only real worry is about receiving a questioning phone call to their office.

> *"Every little action of the common day makes or unmakes character."*
> – Oscar Wilde

The daily grind of coaching and teaching is often filled with what appear to be mundane responsibilities. But in the end, the consistency of those daily disciplines being modeled, taught, and acted out will have far more impact than the occasional large, dramatic ones. The simple, daily lessons learned will last much longer than the championship that will often be forgotten. The degree to which coaches remain persistent and diligent in making a meaningful difference in their players' lives every day is what their athletes will remember most.

Over the years, coaches receive hundreds of small "paychecks" that have nothing to do with money. They receive letters, calls, emails, and meals from former players, as they grow into adulthood and become parents themselves. In all the conversations I have had with former players, I have never had a former athlete call and say "thanks coach for teaching me how to defend a flash post." Instead, the memories former players are most thankful for are the lessons of life that they learned and now live. One of the true joys and benefits of coaching is the fact that the profession of coaching provides an opportunity to change a life...every day.

> *"Those who educate children well are more to be honored than they who produce them; for the latter only gave them life, but the former gave them the art of living well (with moral virtue)."*
> – Aristotle
>
> *"The question to be asked at the end of an educational step is not 'What has the student learned?' but 'What has the student become?'"*
> – James Monroe, fifth president
>
> *"Education does not mean teaching people what they do not know. It means teaching them to behave as they do not behave."*
> – John Ruskin, English author

Great coaches view coaching as a "ministry," not a part-time job. Making coaching a ministry gives more urgency to every minute we spend with young people and gives purpose to the strategies we employ. Viewing coaching as an opportunity and responsibility to instill values, while holding athletes to the highest possible behavioral standards, gives the profession of coaching something that is priceless—eternal value.

CHAPTER 4

Beliefs About Character and Sport

Most philosophy statements are simply belief statements. They begin and end with what the person believes. An athletic philosophy needs both a belief statement and an action statement. Having a philosophy is essential to success, but having a philosophy along with an action statement gives substance and teeth to your philosophical tenets. Sound athletic leadership says with its words and actions, "this is what we believe, so therefore, this is what we will do, and this is what will be seen." Behavioral changes are not always popular at the initial stages of the process with the people or groups who need to make the changes. What you will see will be the behavior of the coaches and athletes as they prepare and compete in a public or private setting. Behavioral choices involving character issues should be one part of every coach's philosophy. This chapter focuses on the action part of the statement establishing an athletic philosophy. This is where most of the work needs to be done, and coaches work in an "action profession."

> "To me, the coaching profession is one of the noblest and most far-reaching in building manhood. No man is too good to be an athletic coach for youth."
> — Amos Alonzo Stagg
>
> "Coaching is the profession of love.
> You can't coach people unless you love them."
> — Eddie Robinson

Young people go through so much of their life surrounded by unmotivated, lifeless people, and then they come to a teacher, clergyman, or coach who lives with passion. Young people deserve our best. They deserve the life in our eyes and the fire in our belly that comes with the coaching profession. Coaching is a profession of eternal value. Coaches are passionate people. Passionate people change lives, change the culture of a school, impact society, and change the world.

The following represents some beliefs on teaching character. You may agree or disagree, but they have been developed by personal experience. If you agree with the belief, you should question yourself concerning where you are as a coach, as a program, or as a school.

Beliefs on Character

❑ Ethical behavior is not something children are born with; it is learned. No one automatically has good character, but everyone is born with the capacity to become good. Everyone chooses his own path when it comes to character. Because character must be taught, coaches should teach their athletes the difference between right and wrong in every athletic situation. This is the primary responsibility of the coach.

❑ Coaches can begin to build character at any age. Small private victories in character development can lead to larger and more public victories.

❑ Some athletic activities are more challenging than others when it comes to displaying correct behavior. In this regard, there are four areas that will cause both the athlete and coach to be more severely tested. The first occurs in games that involve a lot of subjective judgment. The more subjective judgment that the sport involves (i.e., referees' calls), the more opportunities there are for behavioral challenges.

The second factor involves the amount of outside interference. The more things on the outside of the game that come into play, the more likely there are to be problems. Outside interference includes referees, fans, and even coaches. The more the rules allow coaches to be involved in strategies, substitutions, and timeouts, the more potential areas of conflict exist.

The third factor concerns whether the game is a "shared-space" sport or a "barrier" sport. Shared-space sports, such as hockey, football, basketball, and soccer, have all the competitors operating and trying to gain an advantage in the same space. Barrier sports are those that use lanes or nets to divide the participants, such as swimming or tennis. Some sports have a section of the game where space is shared, and if problems exist, they usually happen there. Volleyball has "shared space" at the net. Baseball and softball have shared space in the areas around the bases. Track has shared space in events that are not run in lanes the entire race.

The fourth factor relates to whether contact is allowed or encouraged by the rules. The more physical contact allowed, the more potential for problems.

The most challenging sports that require coaches to be the most proactive are those that have a lot of subjective judgment, outside interference, shared space, and where contact is allowed and encouraged. While all coaches need to work hard to set and hold athletes to specific behavioral standards, coaches in sports like hockey, football, basketball, lacrosse, and soccer have a particular need to understand and anticipate the potential challenges their sports represent.

❑ Coaches who think ethical behavior will be learned just by providing the activity are making a false assumption and are simply leaving character-building lessons up to chance. Expecting character to develop by exposing a person to sport may work for some of your athletes, but often it will only be a perception, based on whether they experienced personal success. Whether an athlete learns lessons of character should not depend on individual or team success. It is important for coaches to remember that an athlete does not have to be "good" to get "good" out of the experience. In this regard, you need to ask yourself the following question: Does the athletic program at your school really teach character or leave it to chance?

❑ Finish this thought…. athletics offers the best opportunities in a young person's life to learn….? Because most people who coach are those who had good experiences as an athlete, the tendency is to automatically think of all the positives that can be learned from participating in sport (e.g., good work habits, teamwork, the importance of obeying rules, honesty, ethical behavior, positive discipline, poise, sportsmanship, etc.).

Participation in sports also offers an equal opportunity to experience and learn the exact opposite of all those good lessons. No easier place exists in a young person's life to learn to cheat than in sport. How many coaches ignore or even teach violations of the rules as "part of the game"? The football player who is taught how to hold an opponent so it will not be detected by an official is learning that cheating is acceptable in some situations. The basketball player who is sent to the foul line instead of the player who was fouled because he is a better free-throw shooter has just learned from his coach that "if you can get away with it, it is fair." Think of all the opportunities that exist for players in almost every game to circumvent rules when no one is watching.

With respect to establishing an environment where your players are exposed to the need to exhibit positive behavior, you need to address certain issues. For example, are your players learning the importance of obeying rules or how to cheat? Are your players learning and demonstrating positive discipline or learning to disrespect authority? Where else can a young person get away with disrespecting authority like they can toward game officials? Go watch any soccer or basketball game involving 10-year-olds, and you will see disrespect shown toward referees, either by players or modeled by adults.

Furthermore, ask yourself the following questions about your players:

- Are they learning good work habits, or how to take shortcuts?

- Are they demonstrating confidence based on preparation, or confidence based on arrogance or a sense of entitlement?

- Are they learning how to handle tough situations with poise, or with revenge, anger, and temper?

- Do they demonstrate the qualities of great teamwork, or are they allowed to be selfish with their effort, attitude, and attention?

- Are they accountable athletes, or have they learned that making excuses is acceptable?

- Have they learned to persevere when things get tough, or have they learned how to quit? Athletics is one of the first areas in our society where young people learn how to say, "I don't like this," or "I'm not getting to play enough," or "this is too hard, so I quit."

Which set of standards are your athletes learning?

CHAPTER 5

Action Statements About Teaching Character Through Sport

The previous chapter examined belief statements. This chapter addresses how you can apply what you have learned. The following sections discuss how to take positive character traits and make them part of your squad selection, practices, and post-games. Because coaches can and should have a huge impact on teaching character as part of their job description, most of the responsibility for teaching character is placed on the shoulders of the coach. As such, good coaches should be able to successfully accomplish this integral portion of their job.

Action Statement #1

The first responsibility of a coach is to lead. You must focus on and do things that need to get done. As the leader of the athletic program (team, school), if you are going to teach character, your underlying precept is, don't be afraid to lead. Leadership is the key component in every successful team.

> *"Great leadership in athletics is like taking eagles and teaching them to fly in formation and like it."*
> — D. Wayne Calloway

Making the decision to truly teach character through athletics on your team or at your school will only occur as a function of sound leadership by the coaching staff. If you inherit or are in a situation that requires change, contrary to popular educational belief, change does not require consensus. Not everyone has to agree to the need for or method of change before it begins. With regard to leadership, you have two critical, challenging issues that you need to address:

- Define your leadership style.

- What do you believe, and do your athletes demonstrate what you believe in?

Action Statement #2

It is essential that coaches lead with respect. Respect can be achieved out of love and honor, or compliance out of guilt or fear. It is up to the coach which path he chooses. Respect generally comes with the title of coach. In many professions, it takes time, effort, and experience to earn the respect of the people working with you. Most young athletes have a level of respect immediately for a coach. If built upon, this level of respect can help promote all the healthy aspects of sport. If you allow the respect that your athletes have for you to diminish, the result can be as bad as a completely negative experience for all involved. As a coach, you almost have to work to not be respected.

A coach, by definition, is the leader of the team. A coach is the authority figure, the person who establishes rules, roles, standards, and expectations. When a team loses respect for its coach, the players will begin to privately, or even publicly, challenge the coach's decisions, strategies, and actions. As soon as that begins to happen, the players can lose focus on the positive direction of the team. Teamwork, effort, attention, and all other athlete-owned behaviors and choices will suffer.

How Do Coaches Get and Maintain Respect?

As stated previously, a modest level of respect comes with the title of coach. In reality, however, there are a number of steps you can take to help maintain and build on the level of respect that players have for you, as their coach. The first step involves having a knowledge base that allows you to understand both the game and the athletes and how to teach *both* equally well. Accordingly, coaches need to continually work to add to the depth of their knowledge, finding ways to teach new skills or strategies, as well as working to improve what they are currently teaching. Athletes will quickly come to understand how much knowledge a coach has to share with them. As a rule, coaches should always have more knowledge at their disposal than they think they will need or choose to teach. Technical knowledge is important, because it is the basis of the skill instruction, but knowledge should also include both the mental and psychological aspects of coaching and learning. The best coaches continue to challenge themselves throughout their careers to improve in every part of their profession.

Keep in mind that higher levels of respect exist that can be achieved by some coaches. The first step to achieving this higher level of respect is to understand and practice making respect a two-way street. Respect needs to be reciprocal. Mutual respect is something that is better demonstrated than talked about. It is done by building a climate of trust and acceptance within the entire program (from coaches to managers). A positive climate of trust and acceptance allows for the steady flow of communication. Good communication includes having players as a contributing part of a well-functioning organization. Interteam communication is honest, open, and appreciated by all parties. Part of the responsibility of a team member is to take both positive and constructive correction as a compliment. Teams have better trust and are more likely to avoid cliques developing when there is common access to information. This factor allows both the coach and the team to stand on common ground and reach for shared goals. A coach demonstrates respect for his athletes by empowering them and giving them credit and ownership when things are done well. Sincere care and love can and should be communicated by showing that you place your athletes above the outcome of the contest.

> *"Either love your kids or get out of coaching."*
> – Bobby Dodd

No more essential ingredient for building a great level of respect exists than *trust*. Trust for most people requires a substantial period of time to develop. In athletics, coaches and players spend an enormous amount of time together. It is not only the quantity of time, but also the sense of urgency and emotion that is attached to the time spent that both tests and builds trust more quickly than normal.

One of the best ways you can tell if a coach is respected by his players is how much failure those players are willing to risk when attempting a new skill in the privacy of practice or playing a game in a public setting. Improvement in athletics, whether it is as an individual or a team, involves challenging yourself to go beyond what you have done before. Improvement always includes some risk and some failure, before success or even new skills are achieved. All factors considered, the more players trust and respect the coach, the more they are willing to risk, and therefore the quicker they can improve. Every coach should remember that improvement will not occur without mistakes. Mistakes are essential for learning. No game is played without mistakes.

> *"Our mistakes don't make or break us. If we are lucky, they simply reveal who we really are, what we are made of. Challenges will come, but if you treat them simply as tests of who you are, you'll come out of it not bitter and victimized, but smarter and stronger."*
> – Donn Moomaw

One of the ways that a high level of trust is established between coach and player is for the coach to develop the ability to differentiate between the types of mistakes. Mistakes made out of carelessness or lack of concentration and those made as part of the learning process that are done with the player's best effort require different types of reinforcement. Coaches develop trusting, respectful, and fearless players if they can find a way to dignify all mistakes made with full attention and full effort.

> *"People are in greater need of our praise when they try and fail than when they try and succeed."*
>
> – Anonymous

When a player is removed from a game for a mistake made at full speed and full attention, the message you send is that they cannot play for you and make a mistake. These players become either so thick-skinned that they play well in spite of you, or they become so tentative they are ineffective. No better time exists for a coach to send a message of trust than after a player has made a mistake. If players get the idea that mistakes made with great effort are alright, they maintain their aggressiveness and perseverance, and are more willing to accept instruction. If you reward great effort, you will get great effort. If you only reward outcome regardless of effort, you are rewarding something you cannot control, and the athlete's effort becomes secondary to the score.

> *"There is a correlation between sustained effort and success."*
>
> – Keith Baker

Mistakes provide an opportunity to teach the character traits of perseverance and being a good teammate. An athlete learns to recover quickly from an error and can assist teammates to do the same.

With regard to the fact that leadership is the key component in every successful team, you need to address the following *challenging* issues:

- *Does your leadership style develop mutual respect?*
- *How much failure are your athletes willing to risk to improve?*
- *Can you dignify all mistakes made at full speed and full attention?*
- *Do your teams play fearlessly?*

Action Statement #3

If you are truly going to teach character through your sport, it is your responsibility (as the coach) to *set and follow through on all expectations*. As a coach, you need to have a blueprint for behavioral expectations (i.e., an exact description of what the finished product should look like).

Good coaches talk about their expectations. Great coaches have athletes who meet their expectations, because these coaches confront incorrect behavior and half-efforts and in doing so, get the love and respect of their athletes.

Coaches who are attempting to teach character in their program can incorporate it during squad selection, game preparation, post-game activity, and awards-and-recognition ceremonies. In sport, it all depends on the coach and whether or not he makes a conscientious effort to actually *teach* the importance of high ethical standards by word, and more importantly by example. Which set of behaviors is going to be learned and demonstrated in the arena is the sole responsibility of the coach. As a coach, you must be able to identify, *teach*, correct, and model ethical behaviors and character traits. For example, you should take the time to teach "poise" the same way you teach any other physical skill that is essential to your sport.

Like anything else you hope to accomplish in a sport, you must *plan for it and teach it* if you want it to happen. Unless you make the effort to teach and correct the character traits that your sport can offer, you cannot say for sure that your sport actually builds character, but rather you are assuming it will happen naturally, and, in reality, leaving it to chance.

Some sport-related situations have an extreme potential for problems. These situations normally involve issues that are real, immediate, and emotional. These problems usually come with a sense of urgency or at unpredictable times that test attitudes and standards and provide moral and ethical dilemmas for all involved. Handling these athletic situations successfully requires actions that not only maintain perspective, but are done quickly and decisively. Coaches seldom have the luxury of time or the opportunity to deal in generalities and concepts when it comes to behavioral problems that occur in the heat of battle. Being an athlete and being a coach is not just what you say, it requires active involvement on the part of everyone. Probably more than any other area of school, or society, action is required. More often than not, values and ethical judgment are at the heart of these actions.

If you are truly going to teach character in sport, you have the responsibility to set and follow through on behavioral expectations. In this regard, you must deal with the following *challenging* issues:

- *What does an athlete look like in your program?*

- *What behaviors that currently exist in your program would you change?*

- *As the leader of your team, what do you want the finished product to look like?*

CHAPTER 6

Teaching Character by Redefining the Term "Athlete"

> *One athlete of character can improve a team.*
>
> — Anonymous

How many times have you heard or even been the one to say "he is really a good athlete"? What does that term "athlete" mean to you? What does it mean to the young people who play for you? Whatever you, as a coach, choose to reward or recognize as being an athlete will be what your players aspire to be. Too often, this comment is directed toward a person who has a high level of physical skill, who moves fluently, scores goals, or is able to make a major contribution to defeat an opponent on the scoreboard. Coaches refer to this person as an "athlete," while overlooking a less-than-best effort or attitude. By doing so, coaches are settling for less than the young person is capable of being. Furthermore, they are also doing this individual a lifelong disservice. Often, the blanket (and shallow) acceptance of this view of being an athlete promotes the feeling that being athletic serves as a guarantee of special privileges. It avoids teaching personal accountability, respecting others, and realizing that sports is only a small part of life. Keep in mind that all factors being equal, young people in your care will meet any standards you establish for being an athlete, either high or low.

Being an athlete is more than having physical skills and more than being able to perform better than an opponent on a certain day. Athletic traits are God-given gifts over which a player has virtually no control. Being an athlete has nothing to do with gender, age, or sport. Being an athlete involves choices you make on the things you do have control over – effort and attitude – in other words, character issues. Please do not consider your players to be "athletes" just because they have been blessed with a particular skill level or ability. Check your players on the seven *character attributes* discussed in this chapter. Hopefully this process will challenge both you and your team members to do some self-examination of the choices they have complete control over, and for which they can be held accountable. As you read through the character traits, continue to ask yourself if these attributes are skills or choices.

With each of the character traits, two descriptions are given:

- One of an athlete or what a great teammate looks like
- A description of a person who has not been taught correctly or learned yet what an athlete or great teammate is

Athletes should examine each of the character traits and decide if they are an athlete under these definitions. Which of the two descriptive options describe them? Do they describe the other people on their team? How would their teammates or coaches rate them? Can they be counted on?

Confidence

What does confidence look like on an athlete?

> *"I fight for my country and my people. When we conquer, I will remain silent like a warrior should."*
> — Lacota Sioux

Athlete

The *athlete* displays quiet, inner confidence based on preparedness—confidence gained from his own preparation and that of his teammates. Genuine confidence is based on belief, and belief is based on consistency of accomplishment and daily work habits. Work habits of an athlete are directed toward achieving excellence of his goals and dreams. This kind of true confidence is contagious within a team. It is a special quality that can be built one athlete to another. These individuals and teams develop an air of relaxed aggressiveness, and of being at ease and comfortable in every situation that may come forward. These athletes can subject themselves to tough challenges and practices and see the value in hard work.

As a coach, are you a confidence builder or confidence cutter? Confidence builders teach young people that confidence and preparation go hand in hand. They lift up their players for their effort to prepare. This kind of coach can reward effort and let the outcome take care of itself, instead of only focusing completely on the outcome of the game. Players are in greater need of our praise when they try and fail than when they try and succeed. Displays of true confidence come out during times of adversity.

Athletes who have learned this lesson play with a sense of relaxed aggressiveness and are unafraid of failure. What a great way to be able to compete! The athlete prepares hard every day, and when success does come his way, he attributes it to the effort he has put into preparation.

Non-Athlete

> *"Egotism is the anesthetic that dulls the pain of stupidity."*
> – Knute Rockne

The player who hasn't learned true confidence tends to be self-absorbed and arrogant. The player with false confidence generally tends to be happy, because the outcome of games proves he has "arrived" and is "entitled," and doesn't have to worry about practicing hard. Having a sense of entitlement may be one of the least favorable attributes that many players develop. Players who have had their skills identified and praised early in their life and have not been held accountable to the same rules or expectations of everyone else learn that their skill level is a key that opens up the door of requiring and expecting "special treatment." Many have learned that they do not have to put the same effort or attention into practices, because "they are the best player." They often develop poor work habits and focus on themselves, instead of their team.

Which description do your players fall under? Are you, as a coach, a confidence builder or a confidence cutter? Have you taught your athletes to have true confidence? Do they play with relaxed aggressiveness, unafraid of failure? Do they attribute their success to preparation or to their "tremendous skill"? Do they remain confident during adversity? In victory do they remain humble and "silent like a warrior should"?

Because having true confidence is a choice, not a talent, coaches can be held accountable for teaching the proper kind of confidence. In turn, athletes should be accountable for demonstrating this type of confidence.

Teachable Spirit

An athlete has a teachable spirit. Do you?

> *"Sometimes it is more important to discover what one cannot do, than what one can do."*
> – Lin Yutang

Athlete

The athlete and great teams have a teachable spirit. In athletic terms, they are coachable. They understand that the coach's job is to identify areas of weakness and help them improve. They also equate correction as a by-product of the coach seeing potential in them to get better. They have learned to *take correction as a compliment.* These athletes look at correction as an opportunity to improve and have enough inner confidence to not feel criticized or singled out. By doing so, they demonstrate a level of true confidence.

What does it mean to take correction as a compliment? What does this situation look like? An athlete, when corrected, gives the coach both verbal and physical cues that he is listening and learning. His body language and voice are saying "thanks for thinking that I am capable of getting better." As a coach, it is your job to make appropriate corrections. It is your way of telling a player that you care about him and think he is capable of improving. In this regard, athletes should worry if they STOP being corrected. That is a sign from the coach that he thinks they are as good as they will ever get, and any form of correction is either wasted energy or will simply lead to frustration.

Non-Athlete

The player without a teachable spirit does not look at correction as an opportunity for growth. This person, who has not learned to take correction, is not a good team member. He often is too self-important to admit he does not know everything. He normally takes any correction as criticism, and has the feeling that he is being "picked on." Usually, any response this player gives is in the form of an excuse. *"It is not my fault – I thought they were going to do it – the ref blew the call – the field was slippery – don't blame me – etc. ..."*

Do any of these descriptions fit you? Do you qualify as an athlete when it comes to taking correction? Are you a good teammate in this regard? How would your teammates describe you?

Keep in mind that having a teachable spirit is a choice, not a skill. Therefore, every player should be held accountable to being coachable.

Pride

What does pride look like on an athlete?

> *"A man wrapped up in himself makes a very small bundle."*
> – Benjamin Franklin

Athlete

Pride is a two-edged sword. On one hand, there is the ego pride, which centers on the individual and his accomplishments, while the "good" kind of pride is a shared feeling. The desirable kind of pride is the feeling between all team members that no one on the outside can understand. True pride becomes "shared joy of the inner circle" of *athletes*. Shared pride involves a desire to become as good as possible for yourself and for the group. It attempts to take ordinary things and make something special out of them. It allows you to be aware of and acknowledge other people and their accomplishments. In this instance, the athlete has pride in the best sense of the word. It is based on:

- unselfishness (they can be counted on)
- and ownership of their behavior (accountability)

In most sports, team pride is developed in the parts of the game that require more effort than skill. For example, in basketball where defense often requires much more determination than technique, teams that have the most "shared joy and true pride" are the ones that compete and consistently stop the opposition on the defensive end of the floor. When it comes to developing the right kind of team pride, determination is more important than talent.

The good kind of pride is never felt by poorly disciplined teams made up of selfish individuals, who play carelessly and without passion. You will never find team pride or a great team when the leadership places individual ability or winning above character.

Non-Athlete

The non-athlete has false pride and says with their words and actions – "look at me, I am great because I happen to win some games or maybe even a championship." This ego-type of pride develops a self-oriented, egotistical image that more often than not is self-defeating. When these people are defeated, they lose their false pride as fast as they gained it. When defeated, "I am great" turns into "we got robbed" or even into a "we-are-no-good" mentality. Their "pride" comes and goes with wins and losses.

The good kind of pride does not include arrogance or entitlement. Unfortunately, you do not have to look very far in the culture of sport to see players who have developed a sense of entitlement. Entitlement occurs when a feeling exists that possessing athletic skill serves as a guarantee of special treatment. Athletes who perceive themselves as entitled feel that normal rules should not apply to them, because they happen to be born with some physical gifts. A sense of entitlement has become the norm in professional sports, but it is often just as apparent in youth sport. Young athletes are frequently coddled by coaches who are afraid to apply discipline for fear that without the individual talent, "they might not win." Young players, who think that they should be excused from practices, paying attention, hard work, or correction, have already developed a sense of entitlement. High school players, who expect exemptions to remain eligible, and professional players, who believe that a large salary and a high skill level allow them to operate above the law, have set themselves apart with their sense of entitlement. Being an athlete should not serve as a guarantee of special privileges.

Parents and coaches need to stop placing their kids on pedestals the day they can execute a crossover dribble or hit a baseball. There are too many homes where success in sports is overemphasized at the expense of sportsmanship and character development. A true athlete understands that he is no better than anyone else, and he acts accordingly.

Developing the right kind of pride is a choice, not a skill. As a player, do you show pride based upon arrogance and entitlement or pride acquired through the shared joy of the inner circle?

> *"It is no great thing to be humble when you are brought low; but to be humble when you are praised is a great and rare achievement."*
> — St. Bernard, Italian Bishop

Integrity

What does integrity look like on an athlete?

> *"Truth has no special time of its own. Its hour is now — always.*
> — Albert Schweitzer
>
> *"The greatest truths are the simplest, so likewise, the greatest men."*
> — Unknown

Athlete

Integrity for an athlete is a simple concept; it is a choice of behaviors displayed in small daily decisions. Athletes engage in actions that follow their worlds and beliefs. In other worlds, their core covenants and their behavior align. Their "yes" means yes, and their "no" means "no." The athlete with integrity says what he means and follows that exact path. His word is good; his handshake confirms the deal, and his signature is worth something.

Non-Athlete

The non-athlete says and signs what is required, and then does what he wants. Teams made up of athletes without integrity have a tendency to self-destruct. Bad character and a lack of integrity are always exposed in a team situation. When coaches focus on ability at the expense of character, they are exposing the team to conflict and confusion within the inner circle and are creating potential problems for society. The model of the coach who focuses on strictly recruiting and developing the physical skills required to "win" games, while overlooking his professional responsibility to teach character and hold his athletes to "standards higher than victory," is one that too often ends up producing outstanding physical performers who are destructive to themselves, their families, and society.

The following story tells volumes about how an athlete's integrity can be a positive reflection on him and his sport. During a recent golf tournament, the television announcers were discussing Tiger Woods. He had driven his ball in the fairway, and it had come to rest in a divot. It was going to take what would normally have been an easy second shot and turn it into a much more difficult one out of a bad lie. One announcer said, "If Tiger would just slightly exaggerate his stance, his left foot would be on a sprinkler head, and he could take advantage of the rule that would allow him to drop the ball to a different and improved location on the fairway." The second announcer simply replied, "Tiger has way too much integrity to do that."

What a tremendous compliment about an athlete. What was said in those few words was that his beliefs are so strong about himself and his game, that he predictably would not even consider gaining an advantage by stretching the rules. Athletes of integrity are the best representatives of their sport, their families, and their society.

Discipline

What is positive discipline, and what does it look like on an athlete?

> *"You can forgive lack of ability, but you cannot ever forgive lack of discipline."*
> – Forrest Gregg

Athlete

Discipline should not have a negative connotation to the *athlete*. Discipline is simply focused attention and effort. And when it is balanced and done through love, discipline is involved in all athletic successes. Other factors being equal, athletes tend to see the bigger picture when it comes to discipline. They understand that in order to be successful individually or collectively, sacrifices involving discipline must be made. Athletes not only accept discipline, they embrace it for the benefit of the team. They have the strength of character to overcome the temptations and pressures and do what is right for their team and themselves at the moment of truth. This attribute is called discipline. The following examples illustrate positive discipline:

- The discipline of attentiveness
- The discipline of enthusiasm and being energized
- The discipline of sportsmanship

- The discipline of respecting authority
- The discipline of personal responsibility

Disciplined athletes accomplish more, have a greater sense of pride, and tend to be better teammates. They are reliable and trustworthy. Discipline involves learning to respect the game, their teammates, the coach, and, most of all, themselves. For the team, discipline is the characteristic that sets them apart and gives them an edge. Coaches should demand discipline from their players, in direct proportion to the amount of love they have for their athletes and the game they coach.

Non-Athlete

For the individual who is not yet an athlete, discipline is normally a dirty word, often associated with a form of punishment. For the non-athlete, this attitude usually results in the player feeling sorry for himself or resisting the intention of the discipline. Lack of discipline is often seen in people who choose self-indulgence over self-control. For many young players, this process involves learning what fun really is. For them, having fun is being silly. They haven't learned to distinguish the difference between discipline as punishment and positive discipline that allows focus and improvement. At some point in the growth of an athlete, having fun becomes being good (skilled) at their particular role.

Another sign of a player who lacks positive discipline is displaying temper. Players should not confuse temper and frustration with being competitive. Temper and frustration are wasted energy. Visible anger can discourage your teammates and give your opponents strength. Emotion, when used in a positive manner, is great, but temper is emotion out of control and eventually will result in damage to both the individual player and the team. Controlling your emotions is not easy; it takes inner strength to redirect your thoughts and actions toward positive attitudes and behavior. Great competitors and true athletes can focus and channel their emotions to help their own performance, as well as the team's.

Accepting discipline is a positive form of teamwork, and it is a choice. Do you appreciate or resist discipline? Are you an athlete when it comes to discipline? Are your teammates athletes, or not?

> *"What we do upon some great occasion will probably depend on what we already are. And what we are will be the result of previous years of self-discipline."*
>
> – H.P. Liddon

Positive Competitive Perseverance

How does an athlete exhibit positive, competitive perseverance?

> *"The man who wins may have been counted out several times, but he didn't hear the referee."*
>
> – H.E. Jansen

Athlete

In athletics, no such thing as a perfect season exists and seldom even a perfect practice. Trouble will always occur with relationships, playing time, winning and losing, and a variety of other constant small setbacks. The *athlete* and great teams are not deterred by bumps in the road. They keep their eyes up. They continually visualize the finished product. The athlete is committed to continuous improvement. He can recover quickly from a mistake and refuse to remain discouraged. The acronym that can be used to remind athletes to recover quickly from a mistake of theirs or a mistake of a teammate is "WIN." It stands for "What's Important Now." By reminding your athletes of "WIN," they know that their responsibility to themselves and the team is to quickly refocus and prepare for the next play.

Each sport has a different recovery time. If he misses an assignment or tackle in football, a player may have 10 to 15 seconds to get refocused in time to give full concentration to the next play called in the huddle. A baseball player only has the time between pitches to refocus. A volleyball player must be recovered and ready by the time the next serve is made. A golfer who hits a bad shot may have five to ten minutes until he must make the next shot. A basketball player who turns the ball over and hangs his head even for a split second may end up not getting back in time to stop an easy basket. As such, athletes must understand their sport and how quickly they must recover to not have a negative effect on their team. Teammates can assist each other to regain their focus by verbally reinforcing "What's Important Now."

A positive and negative side exists to everything. The athlete is able to find a positive side to most situations and bring others with him.

Positive, competitive, persevering athletes are "mentally tough." Young players often misunderstand that term. It is frequently confused with temper, and they interpret being mentally tough with gritting their teeth or pounding a fist on the wall. It is also sometimes incorrectly perceived as having a tough exterior, but really it is having a tough interior. Mental toughness in an athlete is a quality that allows that individual to remain confident, enthusiastic, and positive. Athletes, who are mentally tough, simply cannot have their spirit broken. They can be knocked down, but not out. A mentally tough team can lose to the same opponent ten times and look forward to the next opportunity for a rematch.

> *"A lot of people run a race to see who is the fastest. I run the race to see who has the most guts, who can push themselves into an exhausting pace and then at the end, punish themselves even more. If I lose forcing the pace all the way, well at least I can live with myself."*
> — Steve Prefontaine

> *"A true competitor gets the most joy out of the most difficult circumstances. The real competitors love a tough situation — that is when they focus better and function better."*
> — John Wooden

The *athlete* loves the arena and the game (not the attention). He looks forward to the toughest competition as a test of himself. He wants to compete against his opponent on the opponent's best day. These athletes understand that attitude is a choice and are fully aware that choices are the hinges of destiny.

Non-Athlete

The person who has not learned to be an athlete yet, when it comes to positive, competitive perseverance, gets discouraged easily, and often brings teammates down with him. He allows failures or disappointments that happened yesterday to interfere with today.

As a coach at all levels, I recruited *attitude*. One of the true advantages to the profession of coaching is that at almost every level, you get to choose who you work with. In the classroom, you teach whoever walks through the door. When you get to choose who you work with and who you do not, you learn to watch the small things that offer insight to a player's character. Do not recruit a player who doesn't practice hard. That character flaw reflects a selfish decision to put his needs ahead of the needs of the team, or that he will expect special treatment. Do not recruit a player who is uncomfortable or disrespectful in front of his family. This player will seldom be a good team member. A player who disrespects his coach or teammates in any way, or who doesn't listen during meetings or timeouts, is telling you that he feels he is too important to be coached. Stay away from players who selfishly go after their own goals ahead of team goals — they are "me first" people.

Perseverance and positive attitude are a choice, not a skill. How quickly do you recover from mistakes or failure? Do you bring others down or up with your attitude? Do you love the arena, not the attention, but the challenges?

> *"The secret of success is the consistency to pursue."*
> — Harry F. Banks

Accountability

Athlete

The *athlete* is responsible and demonstrates it by taking personal *accountability* and action for whatever happens to him. The athlete has come to the realization that work and practice are the surest ways to improve. When things are not going well, he looks at himself first to see where he can make a difference. The athlete sees himself as an active participant in his own rescue.

The athlete has the ability to identify and analyze his strengths and weaknesses and develop a plan to bolster his strengths, and at the same time address his weaknesses. Individuals who are *athletes* are problem solvers. They are more likely to be a person who takes initiative. They are more trustworthy and dependable. They are better able to cope with stress and more likely to persevere when facing difficulties.

Non-Athlete

The player who has not learned to be an athlete yet when it comes to accountability will find himself blaming everyone but himself when things do not go well. More often than not, the blame will be directed toward sources out of his control—like the referees, the conditions, the size of an opponent, and the coach. This type of person continues to focus on distractions, while the athlete heads back to the practice floor or the weight room to work on the things that are within his control. The non-athlete consistently sees himself as a victim and is seldom honest with himself about his areas of weakness. He hesitates to tackle his problems head on, preferring to sidestep any responsibility for individual or team improvement.

There is a truism in sports that says, "you are either getting better or you are getting worse." In other words, if you are not making steady improvement, you are losing ground, relatively, to those athletes who are getting better. These non-athletes seldom choose to improve their levels of proficiency above what comes naturally, and usually end the season about where they began skill-wise. They are excuse-makers and blame deflectors, and have difficulty ever admitting that they have made a mistake.

Are you an excuse maker or a problem solver? Are you a victim or a responsible, accountable athlete? Being accountable is a choice that will aid in both individual and team improvement.

Passing the Buck

Said the college professor,
"Such rawness in a student is a shame.
Lack of preparation in high school is to blame."
Said the high school teacher,
"Good heavens, that boy's a fool. The fault, of course, is with the middle school."

The middle school teacher said, "From such stupidity may I be spared.
They sent him to me so unprepared."
The primary teacher huffed, "Kindergarten blockheads all.
They call that preparation? Why that is worse than none at all."
The kindergarten teacher said, "Such lack of training never did I see.
What kind of woman must the mother be?"

The mother said, "Poor helpless child. He's not to blame. His father's folks
were just the same." Said the father at the end of the line,
"I doubt the rascal's even mine."

—Author Unknown

Team First

"There is that interdependence and that strength you get from a team, that the group is greater than any one individual."
– Pete Newell

How does an athlete behave when it comes to being a great teammate?

Athlete

The Native American culture had the concept of "team" figured out, they called it a tribe. A tribe was a band of people who shared a common history, acknowledged a common authority, faced a common danger, and expected a common future. They agreed on what work needed to be done, and who was the enemy.

The Lacota tribe provides a description of a great teammate and "warrior." A warrior didn't try to stand out in a band of warriors, he strove to act bravely and honorably, and to help the group in whatever way he could to accomplish its mission. If glory befell him, he was obligated to give away his most prized possessions to relatives, friends, or the poor.

The process of becoming a good teammate is a decision based on attitude. It signifies a step from independence to interdependence. The *athlete* intentionally puts the needs of the team ahead of himself. He understands that everyone on a team can have different roles, that together can make the team stronger. On a great team, all roles have equal value. The screener is just as important as the shooter in basketball. The offensive lineman who carries out his assignment has equal importance to the running back who carries the ball. The substitute who assists the team to prepare by practicing hard is just as valuable as any starter.

Few experiences will be as helpful in the growth of a young athlete than choosing to be part of a selfless group, working toward a common goal. Though the athletic experience offers many individually satisfying memories, for the true athlete, nothing can compare to the memories built from being part of something bigger than he is.

Teams are relatively fragile and need to be constantly monitored and molded. A wise and creative coach will use everything in his power to provide a "team experience" for his players, and, once accomplished, will give his players proprietorship of the team. Great teams are made up of athletes who have given up their quest for individual glory, who have willingly and wholeheartedly embraced the character traits of a team player, and who have fully committed themselves to the group effort. Being part of a great team will be the athlete's best memory, and building those teams will be the coach's greatest legacy.

Non-Athlete

The player who has not learned how to be an athlete yet when it comes to teamwork looks to satisfy his own needs first by being selfish with his effort, attention, or immature behavior. Non-athletes often look at roles as being limiting and are, at times, selfish with their roles or jealous of other teammate's roles. *You will NEVER see a great team where the most talented players are not the best workers.*

A player who is physically talented and selfish with his effort or level of attention has chosen to be a *selective participant*. A selective participant chooses when he will work and when he will coast, when he will listen and when he will ignore instruction or correction, and when he will focus and when he will tune out. These players usually are last in line, place blame for mistakes on the shoulders of their teammates or coaches, and enjoy having "days off" or "easy practices." They are constantly looking for shortcuts and haven't learned that what you get in life for free is too expensive. They can be described as "wheelbarrows"—they have to be pushed, and they get upset easily. They are team killers and energy sappers. The true athletes on a team do not deserve to put up with these people for an entire season. Unfortunately athletes who have been allowed to behave like this are often the more gifted players. As a coach, you should attempt to do everything in your power to change these players into "team-first" athletes during the off-season. But, if they have not made the choice to be a good teammate by the start of the season, you should not keep them as part of the team. One hard day of cutting these players is considerably better than three or four miserable months with both you and the remainder of the team having to be around them.

Teamwork is a rare gift that allows ordinary people to attain extraordinary results. A team with selfish, self-centered athletes can win games and never feel the benefits of being on "a team." In over three decades of coaching, I only had one rule for my athletes. It was based on the team always coming first in every decision. The rule was, "don't let your teammates down." What does that rule not cover? It encompasses attention, effort, eligibility, decisions on weekends, and leaves the coach wide room for discretion.

Putting the team first and not letting your teammates down in any situation is a choice. When it comes to teamwork, are you an *athlete* or not? Every player should have the opportunity to be part of a GREAT team at least one time in their athletic experience. It can influence who they are for the remainder of their life.

The Challenges That Athletes Face

With regard to making sound choices relating to character, athletes should address the following issues:

- *Is your confidence based on preparation?*

- *Do you have a teachable spirit? Do you take correction as a compliment?*

- *Do you have the good kind of pride? (shared joy)*

- *Do you accept and embrace discipline as a positive statement about yourself, your coach, and your team?*

- *Are you going to be able to stay positive and competitive through the tough times?*

- *Are you a confidence builder or confidence cutter?*

- *Do you take accountability for your own actions? Are you a problem solver or an excuse maker?*

- *Can you accept a role? Put the team ahead of yourself? Can you not let your teammates down in every choice, on and off the field?*

Whose responsibility is it that you make those choices? Your coaches? Your team captains? Your parents? Only you, individually, can make these changes and choices.

Everyone is only an athlete on the field or court for a relatively short period of time. One of the best gifts athletes can give back to a coach, whom they respect and love, is to learn and model the correct lessons from athletics, and then live those lessons in their lives.

Choices for Coachable Athletes

Teams can make a conscious choice to uphold the best of values. Individual players can make choices that will define them as an athlete. Table 6-1 can be used by athletes to evaluate how well they rate on the following attributes:

Enthusiasm
- love of the game
- share it with teammates
- bring it every day

Listening, concentration, and focus
- without this, there is no improvement
- demonstrates respect for coaches and teammates

Selflessness
- the ability to put the team ahead of yourself in every decision
- accept and fulfill a role

Accountability
- to accept responsibility for outcomes
- problem solver, not an excuse maker
- look to yourself first when improvement is needed

Consistency
- reliability
- can be counted on by self and teammates

Work habits
- can subject yourself to hard, productive work
- commit to continuous improvement
- commit to a particular course of action

Discipline
- discipline and love are two sides of the same coin
- accept and embrace discipline for the benefit of the team

- self control on and off the court
- focused attention and effort

Sportsmanship
- respect for the rules and the game
- respect for and accepting the judgment of others
- respect for your opponents as guests
- reacting correctly even when others do not

Determination
- the ability to start your own engine
- quick recovery from mistake–perseveres
- shows initiative
- stay with your obligations and promises

Teachable spirit
- can take correction as a compliment
- consistently seeking new information
- eager to learn

Confidence
- quiet inner feeling based on preparation, not arrogance
- relaxed aggressiveness
- confidence builder

Pride
- shared joy of the inner circle .
- does not require or expect special treatment
- sense of dignity
- valuing the work and accomplishments of the team

Integrity
- purity of intent
- truthful, honorable, and genuine
- being worthy of respect

Competitiveness
- controlled determination
- able to make a quick recovery from mistakes or misfortune

Mental toughness
- inner strength to be able to control emotional responses and concentrate on what has to be done in pressure situations
- use emotion and energy to make yourself tougher, not to give your opponents strength
- nothing can happen that will break your spirit; you stay enthusiastic, confident, and positive

Are You an Athlete?

ENTHUSIASM

1   2   3   4   5   6   7   8   9   10

LISTENING, CONCENTRATION, FOCUS

1   2   3   4   5   6   7   8   9   10

PUT THE TEAM AHEAD OF YOURSELF–SELFLESSNESS

1   2   3   4   5   6   7   8   9   10

ACCOUNTABILITY

1   2   3   4   5   6   7   8   9   10

CONSISTENCY

1   2   3   4   5   6   7   8   9   10

WORK HABITS

1   2   3   4   5   6   7   8   9   10

DISCIPLINE

1   2   3   4   5   6   7   8   9   10

SPORTSMANSHIP

1   2   3   4   5   6   7   8   9   10

DETERMINATION

1   2   3   4   5   6   7   8   9   10

TEACHABLE

1   2   3   4   5   6   7   8   9   10

CONFIDENCE

1   2   3   4   5   6   7   8   9   10

PRIDE

1   2   3   4   5   6   7   8   9   10

INTEGRITY

1   2   3   4   5   6   7   8   9   10

COMPETITIVENESS

1   2   3   4   5   6   7   8   9   10

MENTAL TOUGHNESS

1   2   3   4   5   6   7   8   9   10

AREA OF STRENGTH _____

AREA OF WEAKNESS_____

Table 6-1. A sample rating form for selected character traits

CHAPTER 7

Teaching a Specific Value, Using Themes Based on Character

If you are truly going to teach character in your sport, as the leader, you must examine your sport and decide which life lessons you can naturally teach.

Good coaches understand the game. Great coaches understand the game and their athletes and how to teach both.

Take the time to thoroughly evaluate your sport and discover what characteristics it naturally provides for learning. What life lessons can your sport teach? Does your sport naturally offer the opportunity to both teach and learn …confidence?…courage?…poise?…discipline?…perseverance?…how to win and how to lose with dignity?…teamwork?…how to be a great competitor?…sportsmanship?…integrity?

Identify the qualities your sport naturally can teach and then *put them on the practice-schedule calendar* to be used as themes. They can serve as themes for a day, for a week, or for the season. Just like any other themes you have used in the past, it is going to take some planning, research, and thought to do it correctly and make it meaningful to your team. As a result, instead of working with themes about "take no prisoners" or "kick some butt," you plan around value-oriented themes, such as confidence or courage. With regard to employing themes to emphasize selected character traits, you need to address the following *challenging* issues:

- *What character traits does your sport naturally teach?*

- *Are you leaving them to chance?*

- *Prioritize the top five positive character traits and schedule them into your practices as themes.*

How Do You Teach a Value?

If you are truly going to teach character you must understand how to teach a value. How do you, as a teacher, turn a particular belief into a desired behavior? Coaches have an advantage over most other professions, because most were trained as physical educators and understand the basic rules of motor learning. The rules of motor learning describe how a physical skill should be taught. The recommended steps are to define, model, shape, and reinforce. For example, if you are teaching an athlete to slide into a base who has never done it before, you first define the act, then explain what it is, and finally why you would use it. Next, you show or model what a properly performed slide looks like. Finally, you begin shaping and reinforcing any behavior that comes closer to the desired outcome. Teaching character or values employs the same steps.

Defining

It is important to define character-related traits that you would like to teach as much as possible in athletic terms. The definition needs to be in age-appropriate terms and in verbiage that describes how it relates to your sport. Then, define how the character trait translates into life outside athletics (e.g., to their school, to home, and in society). Before you start defining, it might be interesting to have your athletes identify what different character traits mean to them. Ask them to define the terms and then listen; in most cases, it will alert you to how much work needs to be done. Think how you would define confidence, and then listen to a 15-year-old athlete who has grown up watching WWF, the NBA, or almost any professional athlete on television. Their definition will more than likely involve examples of arrogance, bragging how they think they will do before the game, or making a lot of noise before a game.

By the same token, competitiveness in many untaught, young people will frequently be confused with taunting a beaten opponent, using profanity, or protesting officials' calls. You will often be amazed by the responses of your athletes. In the process, you will see how much work you have to do to get them to understand the true definition of specific character traits.

For some athletes, you may be the first person to teach them what these values actually mean. For athletes who have been trained well at home, you will act as a support mechanism for the character fundamentals their parents have been teaching them.

Your job, as the coach and leader, is to not only change their definitions, but also their behavior when appropriate. If an athlete enters your program with wrong perceptions and actions, that is someone else's fault. They may have been permitted to behave inappropriately by their parents, other adults, or their coaches. But, if they leave your program thinking and acting incorrectly, that situation is your responsibility. With regard to defining the values you would like to teach, you need to address the following *challenging* issues:

• *Write definitions for the character traits you have chosen as themes.*

• *Anticipate how your definitions will differ from those perceptions of the players.*

Modeling

Modeling positive character traits and behaviors involves a description, demonstration, and an exact blueprint of the way you expect athletes to behave in every possible situation. In competition, one of the primary responsibilities of leadership is to minimize the number of unexpected situations that can occur. One of the goals of any coach should be "no surprises." No surprises with the way the team performs or with the players' behaviors. Just like you want your players to practice any offense they are going to run in a game and then execute that offense, you want them to practice and execute correct behaviors to anticipated problems your sport may elicit.

Every sport has some aspects of the game that will test the sportsmanship or character of your players. In order to prepare your players to behave properly when tested, you must identify those problem areas before they arise and then use modeling and rehearsing the behaviors that are acceptable to you as a coach as part of the learning process. As such, you need to consider the following *challenging* matters:

• *Identify potential problem areas for your sport – e.g., officials' decisions, rough play, taunting by an opponent or fan, being substituted for (coming out of the game), striking out, winning or losing at the last second, etc.*

• *Develop a blueprint for behavior that can exactly demonstrate how you expect your athletes to behave.*

• *Devise methods where you can model and rehearse correct behavior before it is needed in an actual game situation.*

Shaping

Shaping may be the most important part of the whole process of teaching not only a physical skill, but also a character trait. Shaping entails having to continue to mold behavior. It involves confronting incorrect behavior with *persistence* and *consistency*. It is an area where coaches should be assessed. It is also a responsibility where some coaches begin to lose their effectiveness later in their career. The ability to persist and continue working to change the same problems year after year is what separates one coach from another and provides for longevity in the profession. If you find that you have lost your ability to persist, feeling like, "I just don't want to deal with that again," then it may be time to consider stepping down as a coach.

There are two facets to shaping as a step in the process to teach a value. The first aspect occurs when things are going well. It includes identification and support of behaviors that come closer to the desired behavior. Praise in any form is the strongest motivator.

The second phase of shaping involves direct, immediate correction of behaviors that are not acceptable. Correction does not have to be negative or threatening to be effective. Correction done in an atmosphere of mutual respect can be given and received as a compliment and an implicit form of love. Direct means you and the athlete are face-to-face. While correction does not have to be done in a public setting, it does need to be one-on-one. Immediate refers to the fact that the correction should be made as close in time to the behavior as possible. It should not be reactionary, rather the sooner the better for the athlete to understand exactly what is being corrected. As a coaching staff, you must identify behaviors that are not tolerable and make a decision about what the consequences will be and then follow through as a group.

As part of the shaping process, think about how you want your players to act and react in every situation your sport presents. Discuss the situations among your coaching staff, making a mental decision to teach the desired value correctly the first time, to correct the behavior when it is not acceptable, and to all agree to react the same whenever possible. This process simply involves being proactive with the ethical dilemmas both coaches and players will have to face. As a coach, you will either be proactive, dealing with situations before they become problems, or you will find yourself having to react after the problems have occurred. If you wait, not only will you be caught by surprise, but problems – certainly unacceptable behavior – will occasionally surface in emotional, public settings involving not the best scenarios for anyone involved.

As a coach, you need to identify not only potential problem areas, but also what behaviors are going to be acceptable and which ones are not acceptable. Almost every year, you can identify a few players in your program who are going to require some changes of attitude or behavior to meet your expectations. Like every other aspect of coaching, it is much better to be proactive with these players. If you can identify and begin working with these players before the season begins, it is very possible they will work at making the positive changes necessary, and you can "catch them" doing things right and give them the first phase of shaping (identification and support). Hopefully, their behaviors can be changed enough that they will reflect in a positive way about the players involved and will never resurface in a negative manner during the season. If you wait until the season begins to identify the people or behaviors, more often than not, you will catch players doing things wrong and then have to take corrective action. Keep in mind that the goal of shaping is to create positive change, not to punish. Some examples of potential behavioral problem areas that apply to almost every sport include:

- Tardiness

- Inattentiveness

- Disrespect

- Less than all-out effort

- Profanity–close to profanity, "coach, I said ship"

As a coach, what behaviors are not tolerable within your philosophy? Can you agree to the same behavioral expectations as a staff within a single program? Can you go further and agree within your entire school? It is extremely beneficial to the players to have consistency of expectations within a coaching staff. If one coach confronts a behavior that another coach ignores, confusion exists and a mixed message is sent to the player.

When it comes to the shaping phase of teaching a value, the overriding truth is that *by not confronting a behavior that is inappropriate, the coach is sending a message of acceptance.* An example of this precept is something that is frequently heard and seen from high school coaches. The coach who states, "I have this crummy group of seniors, and I can't wait until they graduate, but I have this great group of sophomores coming up." Two years later, when the sophomores have become seniors, you hear him say "I can't wait to get rid of these seniors, and I have this great group of freshmen coming in." What has happened is that whatever behavior he has not liked about the seniors has not been confronted to the point of change. As a result, a message has been sent that their behavior is acceptable and part of the right of being a senior. The younger athletes have watched the seniors and think to themselves, "I can't wait to be a senior because they get to come to practice late, listen when it is convenient, coast through practice, etc." The exact opposite can also be true. The younger players might say, "I can't wait to be a senior, because they are the hardest workers, most focused, etc." As a coach, you get whatever you accept and whatever you reward. By not confronting an unacceptable behavior, you are, in fact, rewarding it. In this regard, you need to undertake the following *challenging* tasks:

❏ Establish behavioral standards for your program:

- *Identify what it takes to have you correct (confront) a behavior.*

- *What does it take for you to remove a player from practice?*

- *What does it take for you to dismiss a player from a game?*

- *What does it take for you to remove a player from the team?*

- *Can you become consistent throughout your coaching staff? Your school?*

- *What will you compromise? What will you never compromise?*

❏ Identify any players whom you believe you will need to begin working with before the season begins. Establish strategies for how you are going to change incorrect behaviors, so players that may require behavioral changes do not require removal from participation.

Reinforcement

The final of the four phases of teaching a value involves reinforcement. After you have defined the value and while you are modeling and shaping, you look for any opportunity to reinforce any behavior that deserves recognition. Numerous methods of reinforcement exist. Very simply stated, positive reinforcement results in the strongest change in athletes.

Trust develops more quickly in an atmosphere of positive reinforcement. A coach who uses positive reinforcement as his standard form of communication with athletes can be more direct with all forms of correction. Positive development and character changes occur most easily with trust and affirmation from leadership and teammates. It is a rare coach who can lift his team with both compliments and admonishments, and when this situation does occur, it requires a great deal of established mutual respect.

The greatest management principle concerning motivation is, "whatever gets rewarded, gets done, and will perpetuate itself." The best form of reinforcement is positive, while the best positive reinforcements are verbal, physical, and love. Fear works as a motivator, but does not carry the strength of love and respect. Verbal reinforcement is the most commonly used method by coaches during practice. Your verbal reinforcement can be positive, negative, sarcastic, demeaning, or encouraging. As previously stated, the most effective approach to reinforcement is direct and positive. Effective verbal reinforcement should include both the name and the action of the player you are reinforcing to ensure that the individual receives your full message. Messages such as, "Bill, great job being attentive to the coach when he was teaching"; "Mike, great job running hard"; or "Josh, way to react correctly to a bad situation, well done" carry much more impact than a more general comment, such as, "Good job" or "Good job, Josh."

Reinforcing with Presenters

One of the best ways to combine defining, modeling, and reinforcing (especially) is to bring in presenters to speak to your team. You can dedicate five to ten minutes of practice time at the beginning or the end of a session during which a well-organized presenter can address a desired topic. A well-qualified presenter can bring a wealth of experience or a different perspective to the task. Each presenter needs to understand the theme format you are using and be concise in his thoughts. After you have chosen the character traits that you will use as themes, immediately begin to find and schedule presenters for every theme selected.

Coaches as presenters. Coaches need to be part of every presentation, whether it is introducing the speaker, or the theme, following up with reminders during practice, or actually making the presentation. Coaches are an essential ingredient of the collective efforts to teach values, and should always be present and attentive to the guests at such endeavors. Oftentimes, coaches will conclude practice with a reminder and an opportunity for the athletes to talk briefly on what they have learned about the theme and how it applies to their sport or their life outside the sport. Getting athletes to be comfortable enough to speak out is a process that is best begun in smaller groups, especially if you are coaching a large-group activity (track, football). The head coach needs to continue to pull the themes together throughout the season.

Athletes as presenters. Once you have established themes as a tradition in your program, athletes become more willing to volunteer for an opportunity to present. In fact, times will actually occur when athletes will come in during the spring to sign up for a theme that they know will be presented in the fall. But, when you are just beginning the program, they may be reluctant to volunteer (let alone speak to the group). Encourage your team leaders to respond to the presentation with thoughts of their own or questions. Times will also occur when you may choose to ask a specific athlete to present a designated theme in order to help him see his own weakness and make behavior changes. An athlete, who may be struggling with sportsmanship or poise, can greatly benefit from preparing and addressing those topics in front of his team and coaches if he truly wants to make the desired changes. It is a good idea for the athlete to meet with the coach in charge of scheduling themes prior to the presentation to make sure that the player has organized his thoughts.

Staff as presenters. Having an administrator, faculty, or staff member present once during the week is a great way to build a relationship between your team and the school. It also gives the presenter some insight and appreciation for what you are trying to do for the athletes' lives outside of simply playing the sport and winning games. The presenter sees what you do in your arena and tends to develop an appreciation for the amount of preparation, emotion, and energy it requires to coach.

You will be surprised how flattered people are to be asked by an athlete or coach to address the team. Often, athletes are asked to nominate the teachers whom they would like to have speak to the team. It is a good idea to have players nominate individuals whom they respect for their ability to teach, and then approach the teachers from that perspective. After a staff member has made such a connection with the team, a number of beneficial by-products are often seen, including an improved relationship between student-athletes and teachers, increased attendance at games, better communication in class, and enhanced level of communication between teachers and coaches—all of which are good for the school climate.

Community members as presenters. We have had tremendous success with having members of the community presenting. There is usually a wealth of talent in your community to draw from. Clergymen, ex-athletes, people who have overcome adversity, community leaders, and parents have all been effective.

Former athletes as presenters. One of the steps that you can take to form a historical connection with your program is to have former athletes come back and present to the current players. Such a practice can quickly become a treasured tradition. Establishing valued traditions is one of the key components to building successful teams. Developing any kind of positive tradition always gives the athletic experience additional value, and provides your program some enhanced sense of "history." Former athletes are usually able to relate to the current players, understand the goal of the themes, and may be able to express how the value of learning the lessons from their sport experience has assisted them as they have grown into adulthood. This process also helps develop a tie between generations of athletes. Furthermore, this approach can help the current players realize how they will be respected for what they have accomplished by the players who will follow them.

Reinforcement through Spotlighting

As a coach, your words have power. Your words can build up individuals and teams, stand with time, and create memories. Your words will categorize you as either a confidence builder or a confidence cutter. There is also real strength in the sincere comments from one teammate to another. Words coming from the right person, at the right time, can go directly to the heart.

> *"Words do not last long unless they amount to something. It does not require many words to seek the truth."*
> – Chief Joseph of the Nez Perce

Spotlighting is a form of public praise. It is done by having one teammate or coach make a positive statement about another in front of the group. Time can be set aside to spotlight before, during, or after practice, or before or after games. When your athletes become comfortable speaking about one another in public, it can also be a good idea to allow parents, former team members, friends, extended family, or staff to come to the post-game session. Spotlighting must be specific to the theme that is being featured that week; only athletes and coaches should speak; and every player does not have to be recognized for the procedure to be successful. An example of post-game spotlighting would be to have the coach identify a player for something the athlete has done that week that models the character theme, for example, "I would like to spotlight Jim for the *unselfishness* he showed in practice by being willing to accept the role of a new position." In turn, Jim then "spotlights" a teammate for an example of unselfishness. Each player needs to give some forethought about whom and what he would spotlight in case he is called upon. The coach can allow the comments to go as long as they are meaningful, sincere, and on target. Public praise occurs in a situation where positive individual behavioral changes can be recognized, as well as when coach/player, player/player relationships develop.

Reinforcement with Inspirational Quotes and Messages

The character themes of the week can be reinforced with the use of inspirational quotes and messages. Well-chosen words can carry distinctly different messages to each player. Words initiate thoughts, thoughts provide motivation, and motivation produces action.

A meaningful message sent or delivered by a personal note or placed on a bulletin board in the locker room can spark positive thoughts and actions. Many great quotes and stories exist that will reinforce the personal-character-trait themes. At the conclusion of practice, it only takes a minute or two to discuss the meaning of the quote chosen for "today," but the value of another reinforcing message of the character theme may stay with the athlete for a lifetime.

Reinforcement with a "Wall of Fame"

Referring to previous discussion concerning the theory on motivation that states that, "whatever you reward, you get, and it will perpetuate itself," it is wise for you to use as many different models of reinforcement as possible. Everything you do as a coach reinforces to your players what is really important to you. One of the easiest methods of reinforcement is to keep and post pictures of former athletes who have learned and demonstrated the character traits you expect from your athletes. This simple process will help encourage your current athletes to emulate the desired behaviors by enabling them to see who is a special player in your past. Players or teams who are on your wall should reflect the desired level of *character*, not ability. Memorializing individuals who demonstrated the character that you are striving for sends a strong message of what is important to you as a coach and may help influence a player or team in choosing the right path.

Reinforce, Using Character-Related Awards

Whatever you choose to recognize in terms of personal accomplishment states very clearly where your priorities are as a coach. When you give an award for "Most Valuable

Player," it usually goes to a player with a high level of talent. If you can also find a way to reward players who demonstrate character that make the team better, it may more clearly define what is important to you and perpetuate the desired behavior in more players. In this regard, as a coach, you need to address the following *challenging* issues:

- *Identify what forms of reinforcement you currently use.*

- *Identify and contact people on your staff or in your community who can be presenters.*

- *What awards can you give to reward positive team behavior or character?*

Developing a Theme

Themes can be for the day, week, or year. For example, some years we would select a different theme for each week. Other years we would take five to ten different themes for the first two weeks, and then come back during the game schedule and revisit five or six key themes in more depth, doing one per week building up to the game(s).

The following example demonstrates a method that can be employed to teach character with the theme of courage. Courage is a theme that can be taught naturally within a sport such as football, for example.

In our situation, once we selected courage as our theme, it was scheduled for a specific week and important game of the season, and we began locating presenters for that week and topic. The first day of the week at a pre-practice meeting, we asked players to *define* courage. As with other character traits, we found that our players' perception of courage was something that needed adjustment. Real courage is not something that needs to be dramatic or newsworthy or demonstrated only in the physical parts of a game, but can often be seen in small decisions and choices that individual people make on a daily basis, for example, doing what is expected of you, when you are being counted on within the team.

Courage can be demonstrated in decisions when you are alone or in the presence of witnesses. Choose the higher path, even when others are making poor decisions, regardless of the perception that "everyone else is doing it." Courage can be found in many places and with people who are fighting battles different than your own. It can be demonstrated by practicing hard, by being reliable when no one is watching, by continuing to try when you are not immediately successful, and by disciplining yourself to stand alone if necessary with your personal beliefs (e.g., avoiding peer pressure). Once real courage has been redefined in terms like that, athletes begin to recognize courage in their lives and in the lives of those around them. Athletes often come to understand that most people have far more courage than they have given themselves credit for, and, once discovered in themselves, acts of courage are easier to repeat.

Once this kind of courage is seen in others (i.e., teammates and family), courageous choices are more recognized and appreciated.

After having courage defined by players and coaches, other presenters continued the process of further defining the desired trait, and began modeling, shaping, and reinforcing the theme. Players were reminded, for example, that there were examples of people with courage all over their community. When opportunities presented themselves in practice, we had players or coaches name an act of courage that they had witnessed, in practice or around school. Throughout the week, the coaches looked for opportunities for continuous reinforcement of courage as a theme by effectively using presenters, examples, and written messages. The following examples illustrate different quotes that we used when the theme of the week was courage.

> *"Being courageous requires no exceptional qualifications, no magic formula, no special combination of time, place, and circumstances. It is an opportunity that sooner or later is presented to all of us."*
> – John F. Kennedy

Former president Kennedy's quote reinforces the idea that courage does not have to be some dramatic event, rather that courage is something that we are capable of, and have a responsibility for, when it is required.

> *"We need people who influence their peers and who cannot be detoured from their convictions by peers who do not have the courage to have any convictions."*
> – Joe Paterno
>
> *"One man with courage is a majority."*
> – Andrew Jackson

These quotes serve as a great reminder that players can stand with their own beliefs and do not have to follow the crowd.

In our situation, times occurred when we sent the entire team the same quote and discussed its meaning at the conclusion of practice. Other times, we sent each player a different quote on the same theme and asked for individuals to speak who found special meaning in their particular quote.

We then used spotlighting as a reinforcement tool. We concluded practice by talking about the quote for the day and then opened up the discussion for two or three quick spotlights of examples of courage in the players' teammates. In the five-to-ten minute post-game meeting during the week when courage was the theme employed, the following actual examples of spotlights identifying courage were given:

- Identification of courage based on small but significant changes and choices
- Being at practice and giving your best when ill
- Trying out for football for the first time
- Taking correction
- Not quitting
- Raising your hand and asking for help in math
- Walking away from a situation during the weekend that "could have gotten us all in trouble"

Summary Points

Among the challenges that coaches face with regard to using a theme to teach a specific value are the following:

- *Decide what you believe, and then live it through your coaching model*
- *Don't be afraid to lead*
- *Do not hide your passion or apologize for it*
- *Be a positive model in the lives of your players on a daily basis*
- *Don't leave the learning of character to chance. Choose, plan, and teach the values your sport naturally provides.*
- *Be a coach who gives his profession eternal value.*

Coaching needs individuals who love kids enough to hold them to high standards, challenge other adults to be accountable, and enlarge the athletes' expectations of themselves. One major responsibility as coaches should be to teach athletes to think and act correctly. Behavior (good or bad) cannot be hidden; it is available for public view and scrutiny. However, it is not for the purpose of public perception that you should teach honorable behavior in your athletes. You should teach it because it is what they remember long after the last game is won or lost, and it is truly what gives the profession of coaching eternal value. The changes athletes make in their life and the values they learn to practice from an experience with this kind of coach will make a difference in the kinds of families and communities they help build in the future. It is not a choice that great coaches have. If you sincerely love your athletes, you will teach and hold them to the highest possible behavioral standards.

At the conclusion of your coaching career, you will not be defined by personal accomplishments, winning percentages, or possessions, but by the impact you have had on the lives of other people, namely your players. This reality is why teaching and coaching is a special, fulfilling profession of eternal value. Your coaching legacy will be the teams you have built, the passion you have shared, and the lives you have changed.

> *"Be the change you want to see in the world."*
> — Gandhi

CHAPTER 8

Teaching Character by Practicing Sportsmanship

The act of sportsmanship involves many character traits. At a minimum, it entails making value choices about poise, respect, discipline, confidence, and integrity. Nearly any behavioral or ethical problems that arise during competition fall into the category of unsportsmanlike behavior. Sportsmanship is not a passive activity of acceptance. It is a positive statement that an individual athlete or team is disciplined enough to maintain perspective and poise, and is willing to do what is best for his teammates.

The behavior of your players during competition is often a very public reflection of your school and the coach. Like it or not, athletes are on a public stage, being critiqued by everyone in attendance. But even more important than the reaction from others is the opportunity that athletics has to reveal personal character to the athlete himself. This situation may offer the only place in a young person's life where he is under such scrutiny and has a chance to model what he has learned. Every game and every practice provide a test for each player to win or lose with class, to learn to accept decisions made by others, and to do what is right, regardless of other influences. Not only is a player given a chance to do what is right, but to do it in public, and at the moment of truth.

So many of the poor behaviors that occur are thought to be "part of the game," emanating from a logical attempt to gain an advantage. Some people believe if you are able to gain that edge, it excuses you from obeying rules and traditions of the sport.

Not surprisingly, many players feel that "it's only cheating if I get caught." In reality, a distinct difference exists between gamesmanship and sportsmanship. The former is only concerned about the outcome of the game at any cost, while the latter involves playing within the rules of the game to determine who is the better team on that day.

Teaching and demanding that your athletes make the correct behavioral choice are the sole responsibility of the coach. Your athletes will tend to do what you tolerate. As such, you should emphasize to your players that the honor and ethics of their sport are dependent on sportsmanship.

When preparing your teams for the season, you should rehearse as many of the physical and mental situations that they might have to face as possible. You should never think about putting a team on the floor or field that is not prepared for such occurrences as:

- Any potential defense or offense they may face

- End-of-game situations

- Onside and anti-onside kicks in football

- First-and-third situations in baseball

- Shoot-outs in soccer

- Etc., etc.

Most coaches usually take time early in the season to talk about how they expect their athletes to behave in certain situations. However, just like with all the other aspects you attempt to prepare your team to perform correctly, talking is not enough. As the coach, you must talk about it, describe it, model it, practice it, and correct the desired behavior. The final step is to enforce the behavioral expectations you have established by following through with disciplinary steps when necessary.

In other words, you must put sportsmanship in your practice plan if you expect your athletes to make the correct behavioral choices. This is the pro-active approach to facing such situations. Each coach must take the time to identify the potential problem areas involved in his particular sport (e.g., line calls, striking out, language, referees' calls or non-calls, rough play, winning and losing, taunting, substitutions, etc.). For example, if you are a baseball coach, how do you want your players to act when they strike out with the bases loaded in the last inning? How do you want them to respond when they hit a game-winning home run in the same situation? Subsequently, you should develop an exact blueprint of how you want your athletes to respond at those times and practice them.

Every sport offers unique opportunities to exhibit good or bad sportsmanship. Each coach has the responsibility to take corrective action and to prepare his athletes in practice before they take the stage. If you wait until the game has actually begun, most of your correction will be punitive in nature.

Within a staff, the coaches should be consistent in their expectations and agree on what behaviors they will and will not accept from their athletes. After you have identified every potential problem area and have developed a blueprint of the appropriate response, you need to get agreement from all of the coaches in your program concerning what constitutes acceptable behavior, what behavior will not be tolerated, and how such behavior will be dealt with. After describing the situation and reviewing both acceptable and unacceptable responses to the team, you should create situations in practice that allow your athletes to practice their responses and have those responses evaluated like any other skill you are trying to teach.

Example of Rehearsing Sportsmanship During Practice

The following scenario illustrates an example of how we attempted to rehearse sportsmanship during our practices. As a former basketball coach, one of the areas I identified where our athletes needed to behave correctly involved responding to referees' decisions. In order to practice this behavior, we chose a time prior to the first game where we had referees at a scrimmage. After several quarters of action, we had a break in which I quietly asked the referees to make a lot of "wrong" calls during the next few minutes of the scrimmage. If it was a block, call it a charge; if blue hit it out of bounds, give it back to blue; call three in the key or any travel or dribble violation they wanted to, whether it occurred or not. (The referees loved it.)

The results were very insightful. After about five minutes of "wrong" calls, we stopped the action and called the team together with the two referees and explained what we had asked the officials to do. Then, we asked the players how they thought they had done, since we had intentionally not corrected any of their actions during this part of practice. Next, we went to videotape of that section of practice and replayed it for the players to see. Some players had responded correctly, while others had not. It was all there for everyone to see. It was an opportunity to kind of laugh at ourselves, but still to take it seriously enough to acknowledge those who had responded correctly and correct those who had not. It also gave us a non-threatening way to discuss what the repercussions would be if that had happened in a game, or even in practice. Later, we were able to speak privately with those athletes who were the most out of line. Again, we used the videotape that showed close-ups of faces after a call had been made, so the individual player could watch his response. These players were the most temperamental and the ones we worried most about, and by bringing them in by themselves, it preserved some dignity that may have been lost by too much public correction. It allowed them to admit that they did not want to react that way, and that it was indeed detrimental to the team.

The same technique could be used to test or practice any of the other responses you expect your athletes to make during the heat of competition. Scenarios, such as rough play, entering or leaving a game, winning or losing, can all be practiced. If it is important to you how your athletes respond when they are in public, then you must practice in the privacy of your team setting.

The profession of coaching is an awesome privilege and responsibility. A quality athletic experience should make a significant contribution to the life of each individual participant. For those students without the benefit of a religious presence or a strong family, athletics may be their last best hope to be exposed to the need for having a values orientation in their lives. Their strong desire to play and please both their coaches and teammates provides some of the best leverage to teach lessons that will last much longer than any physical skill or undefeated season could possibly endure.

Your athletes will find that they can compete as hard as anyone you will ever meet, but by being sincerely humble, they can drive away arrogance. By developing quiet confidence, they can neutralize anger. By modeling true sportsmanship (doing what is right, regardless of the situation or what others may be doing), they can be an agent to help adjust the culture of sport. Athletically, they may be the only good example for the next generation of athletes. How clear will their message be?

With regard to sportsmanship, as a coach, you need to address the following *challenging* issues:

- *Identify the most common areas of your sport where unsportsmanlike behavior can occur.*

- *Make a conscious decision of exactly how you expect your athletes to respond (e.g., what will be the correct responses, and what will be unacceptable, and what the consequences will be for those actions).*

- *Set up sessions in practice to test the responses of your athletes before they get tested in competition. Provide your players with a chance to practice responding correctly.*

- *Make a point to identify, practice, and reward positive sportsmanship behaviors.*

PART III

Crafting a Team

"Ten strong horses could not pull an empty baby carriage if they worked independently of each other."

— John Wooden

CHAPTER 9

Qualities of Great Teams

> *"Teamwork makes the dream work."*
>
> – Anonymous

If you have ever experienced the miracle of being part of a great team as either a player or a coach, it is something that you will always remember. Making a team a great team involves certain choices that are in the control of the participants. Building a team involves believing, becoming, and belonging. Few experiences can be as powerful in the growth of young athletes as being part of a selfless group, working toward a common goal.

Many coaches look at team spirit as an intangible factor that some teams have and others do not. As a coach, it is your responsibility to teach, promote, and build this attribute, and not leave it to chance. As such, you must use every bit of your creative energy to develop team spirit within your players. You must find opportunities to encourage teamwork and unselfishness every day. Though many great personal relationships are fostered through athletics, your favorite memories will often be of your seasons where a group of individuals under your guidance developed into a special team. Such a team learned the lessons you were trying to teach. In the process, your players accomplished goals together that they could have never done by themselves. By correctly applying all the essentials for team-building, a coach can enhance the worth of the team many times the sum of its individual parts.

> *"Regardless of personal accomplishments, the only true satisfaction a player receives is the satisfaction that only comes from being part of a successful team."*
>
> –Vince Lombardi

The satisfaction of building teams and changing the lives of your individual players in the process may be the most gratifying experience coaching can offer. As their leader, you have demanded commitments and a level of excellence from them that has allowed them to achieve things that they may have thought were not possible. Getting a group of people to blend together and achieve greatness is an experience unique to only a few professions. Coaching often serves as the model for other professions as they try to bring a "team" of people toward a common goal. For example, look at how many of the terms that coaches use are now popular in the business world, as businesses attempt to create a productive and cohesive atmosphere in the workplace.

Team-building is an exercise of passion for coaches who love their job. Coaching a great team is the next best thing to being an athlete in that situation. The steps involved in building a team are consistent and predictable. These steps are parallel to any situation that involves developing a cohesive group to work together to pursue a common goal, whether it is building a team in sport, business, or in life.

The professional histories of most coaches stem from the teams with which they have been associated. One of the best examples of this point is Colonel Red Blaik, who coached the great Army teams at West Point more than five decades ago. In answering the question of why a person would want to be a coach, Blaik said, *"Once in a while you are lucky enough to have the thrill and satisfaction of working with a group of young men who are willing to make every sacrifice to reach a goal and then experience the achieving of it with them. In this, believe me, there is a payment that cannot be matched in any other pursuit."*

Eight Qualities of Great Teams

Over the years, every sport has witnessed its share of great teams. While recognizable differences between these teams certainly existed, a number of common traits can also be identified. These commonalities suggest that no matter the sport or the competitive level, certain qualities tend to elicit greatness in teams. In that regard, this section addresses the following eight qualities of great teams:

- Leadership
- Guiding principles
- Pride
- Communication

- Motivation
- Persistence
- Role players
- Positive attitude

❑ **Great teams have strong *leadership*:**

> *"The power of we is greater than the power of me."*

Sound leadership on a team requires several factors. The two best terms to describe the characteristics necessary for good leadership in athletics are *relaxed aggressiveness* and *positive demanding*. A sense of urgency exists about factors that are really important. Effective leaders have the ability to separate the essentials from nonessentials. They do not waste their energy and attention on matters out of their control or on matters that are not essential for team success. They are demanding without being demeaning. They are relaxed and confident, while maintaining a naturally competitive personality. They focus positively and aggressively on factors that they can actually influence.

Coaches generally fall into one of two categories – they either rationalize problems or they accept responsibility for problems. Those who continually deflect personal responsibility for problems seldom improve as either a coach or leader. Positive, responsible coaches look at themselves first when things are not going well. The following six precepts reflect the essential nature of sound team leadership:

- *Leaders of great teams develop loyalty.*

> *"When you get to where you are going, the first thing you do is take care of the horse that got you there."*

True leaders are chosen to *serve others*. Trouble always exists when the leader forgets this concept and begins to serve himself. The two main focuses of leadership need to be (1) the well-being of the team members and (2) the task(s) everyone associated with the team is attempting to accomplish. By creating a climate where members of the team feel valued, positive connections are established at all levels of the group.

Loyalty is tested most when things do not go well and the resultant challenges seem to be somewhat overwhelming. When roles have been embraced, the covenant of great work habits established, and a "team-first" attitude is the norm, the best of teams have an atmosphere of unconditional acceptance. An unspoken feeling exists between all members of the group that "you can count on me, I will be there for you." The power of loyalty is the force that brings out a team's best qualities during the time it is most needed.

> *"Regard your soldiers as your children, and they may follow you wherever you may lead. Look upon them as your beloved sons, and they will stand by you unto death."*
>
> – Sun Tzu

- *Leaders must see the big picture.*

> *"You can't stop at every barking dog or you'll never get the mail delivered."*
> — Phog Allen

Great leaders are capable of consistently moving their team toward a shared vision. Leaders need to keep their eyes up and constantly visualize the final product. They cannot be deterred, distracted, or derailed by insignificant details or small bumps in the road. They do not coach against an opponent, as much as they coach against a vision of how good they think their own team can be. They then are able to take the necessary steps to make their vision a reality. They set challenging goals for their team daily, weekly, for the season.

- *Leaders focus on the things that need to be done and do them.*

> *"In matters of principle, stand like a rock; in matters of taste, swim with the current."*
> — Thomas Jefferson

Effective leaders are not afraid to lead or to change when change is needed. They do not shy away from challenges or responsibility. They refuse to exist in a climate of apathy or to give less than their best effort. They do not second-guess themselves on decisions made with integrity, thoughtful intelligence, and with the heart of the team placed first.

> *"An army of deer led by a lion can defeat an army of lions led by a deer."*

When a conflict arises, successful leaders manage it quickly and effectively. This approach enables the team to maintain its confidence, energy, and collective power. When real change is needed in a situation involving coaching and athletics, it does not require consensus. A leader who sees that change is needed does not have to receive the approval of everyone involved to create the change. A coach who inherits players whose behavior is poor does not have to get the approval of the players to get them to behave correctly.

- *Leadership needs to be positive.*

> *"Athletes want a model, not a motto."*

Positive leaders identify people who are doing things well and reinforce the action or behavior. Perhaps, the best term that can be used to describe successful coaching is *positive demanding*. Positive leaders focus on what kids CAN do and not on what they

CANNOT do. While they continue to work to have their athletes improve their weaknesses, they also stress their athletes' strengths.

Leaders are either confidence builders or confidence cutters. Athletes, like most other people, are in greater need of your praise when they try and fail than when they try and succeed. Make sure that your team members know they are working with you, not for you. Real leadership is needed and revealed during times of adversity. Rather than dwell on failures, good leadership highlights talents, accomplishments, and provides positive feedback, and in doing so, breeds confident teams. Leaders have a quiet inner confidence based on readiness and their ability to prepare others to accomplish the tasks at hand. True confidence is gained from productive preparation and is spread by confident leadership.

- *Leaders go the extra mile.*

> *"Rings and jewels are not gifts, but apologies for gifts.*
> *The only true gift is a portion of thyself."*
> — Ralph Waldo Emerson

Emerson's quote is especially relevant to the profession of coaching. The best way that I can describe the concept of going the extra mile is to relate a true personal story about legendary UCLA basketball coach John Wooden.

A Lesson in Humbleness from the Greatest Coach

In the early 1970's, I was a young coach attending a coaching clinic in Seattle primarily to hear John Wooden. As I listened to him speak, I realized how much of my own personal philosophy I had developed from reading, listening, and observing him.

As I sat there, I said to myself, I just need to go shake his hand and tell him thanks. As he concluded his presentation, I made my way out to the hallway, hoping to get a chance to meet him. Obviously, many of the other coaches in attendance had the same idea, and I found myself last in a long line of coaches. I waited, growing more nervous as the line shortened. When it came my turn to talk to Coach Wooden, I introduced myself as "Bruce Brown, a coach at Hyak Junior High, Bellevue, Washington." In the excitement of the moment, I do not remember much else of what I said, except something about using his "Pyramid of Success" for our football and basketball players. He seemed genuinely interested and sincere during the short conversation. The entire interaction could not have lasted more than two minutes, but as I drove home in my Volkswagen bug, I was about twenty feet off the ground, just shaking my head thinking I had really talked to John Wooden.

About two weeks later, I received a letter addressed to, "Bruce Brown, Bellevue Junior High, Bellevue, Washington," with a UCLA return address. Inside the envelope was a copy of the "Pyramid of Success," signed, "Best Wishes, John Wooden." Needless to say, I placed it in a frame I could afford as a beginning teacher and put it in a safe place.

As I have thought back over the years, I am amazed at many small, but significant, lessons that were demonstrated during that period of time. First of all, Coach Wooden had the courtesy to stay afterward and personally greet every coach who wanted to meet him. How different is it today when "big-name coaches" are brought in and exit by a side door so that people in attendance will not bother them. Secondly, the greatest coach of our generation had listened to what I had to say, remembered what we talked about, remembered my name, and approximately where I taught. Finally, he took the time to sign a copy of the "Pyramid of Success" and mail it to me. What a great lesson in humbleness, from the greatest coach of all time. This lesson has stayed with me through three decades of working with young people. I have continued to keep the copy of the Pyramid in the same inexpensive black frame to this day. It reminds me to always be available for players who need individual assistance or just time.

The professions of teaching and coaching have such eternal value. We have daily opportunities to go the extra mile, to demonstrate humbleness, to aspire ourselves and inspire others to greatness. Thanks Coach Wooden for being a model of that value for so many educators in our generation.

- *Great teams have quality leadership from their team members. The most talented players should be the best workers and have a teachable spirit.*

A teachable spirit simply means that the athletes with this attribute have learned to take correction as a compliment and that the coach believes in them and cares that they reach their full potential. If your most talented players are not your best workers, you will never have a great team. If a coach treats players with a low effort the same as those with high effort, the message is sent to every athlete in your program that high effort is not important or essential for success.

On some teams, you may be a leader; on others, you may be a team member or a role player. Within a school, some of the best "teams" may have nothing to do with athletics. The best functioning teams may be a group of individuals involved with the performing arts, the student senate, or even a single classroom led by a great teacher. Whenever possible, the coach should turn some of the team's leadership over to qualified team members. Some years, the coach must assume all of the leadership responsibilities. Frankly, this scenario is not as effective or fun. It requires a lot of extra energy and can lead to burnout. Having athletes take ownership of the team teaches them that they have been recognized as filling a responsible role for the team and also gives the coach time and energy to achieve other goals.

❑ Great teams have *guiding principles*:

A sound, professional philosophy guides and supports everything the team does and stands for. What does your team stand for? What is the identity of your team? What are you known for? If you were to produce a one-minute video snapshot of your team, what would it say? Too often, philosophies or mission statements look good in writing, but are not who you really are …what do you really believe about your team?

In my case, the guiding principles of my teams remained the same for the three decades I actively coached, regardless of age of the athletes, gender, or sport. The basic foundation of our program and the guiding principles that we encouraged and adhered to were *enthusiasm, work habits,* and *a "team-first" attitude.* Without these principles being consistently in the forefront, nothing meaningful would have gotten accomplished.

• *Enthusiasm.*

> *"I am the greatest builder in the world. I am the foundation of every triumph. No matter what your position is, I can better it. My name is enthusiasm."*
> – Anonymous

Great teams demonstrate enthusiasm. Enthusiasm is both powerful and contagious. It provides the energy for your athletes to be better workers, who in turn will produce a better product. Coaches need to be able to teach the fundamentals, but also be able to teach and model how to love the game, as well as prepare their teams to excel. It is very difficult to excel in any activity that you do not love. What a great gift for young people to learn to put their heart into their work and to not be embarrassed to let it show. Most athletes bring a high level of enthusiasm to the athletic arena every day. In reality, enthusiasm can be spread. As such, having athletes identify it in each other can be one of the quickest methods of spreading the fire. Coaches need to bring their own love for the game, for the players, and for teaching with them to every practice. The coach who has a positive, aggressive approach to his job each day can become a model of a determined, strong-spirited optimist for his players to exemplify.

• *Work habits.*

> *"One day of hard practice is like one day of clean livin' – it won't help."*
> – Abe Lemons

Great teams display excellent work habits. Teams tend to be successful when the athletes prepare hard every day, and then, when success does come their way, they attribute their success to preparation. In athletics, most successes and defeats can be traced to preparation. Every game is an opportunity to measure yourself against your own potential; but every practice is an opportunity to prepare your potential. Preparation is one of the areas of sport over which every coach has complete control. A wise coach only focuses on the controllable factors.

> *"Most battles are won before they are fought."*
> — Sun Tzu (450 BC)

Your goal should be to outprepare everyone on your schedule. How you work, how much you concentrate, how much effort you expend, and how much planning you do are choices. Develop the feeling on your team that practices are not intended to prepare you against a specific opponent, but rather a chance to prepare to fully develop the potential of your team. Once prepared, you then are ready to play whoever arrives on your field or gym on a given day.

- *Team-first attitude.*

> *Teamwork is a rare gift that allows ordinary people to attain extraordinary results.*

The final guiding principle is that *the team should come first* in all decisions. Having too many rules will often inhibit, rather than improve, leadership. It turns the coach into an interpreter of rules, instead of a leader of the team. He becomes more of an "administrator" or "manager," than a leader/coach. Many "administrators" set and follow rules to keep them from having to make decisions. At one time or another in their careers, most coaches have been associated with school administrators who hide behind rules to avoid being accountable. The written rules allow them to not have to make a decision that is based upon their own judgment or leadership. Effective leaders are not afraid to use their discretion to make decisions and then take full responsibility for them.

One of the first responsibilities of successful team leadership is to eliminate selfishness. Selfishness on the team level or with any individual player will destroy a team faster than anything else.

❑ **Great teams develop *pride*:**

> *God opposes the proud, but gives grace to the humble.*
> — James 4:6

Neither teams nor members of teams should confuse pride with arrogance or a sense of entitlement. The kind of pride that helps build a team involves a feeling between all participants that no one not connected to the team can fully understand. This kind of pride is based on discipline (focused attention and effort), unselfishness (the team comes first), accountability (individuals can be counted on), and ownership of their collective behavior. Successes are shared, trust established, communication is kept open, and new members are welcomed in as soon as they understand and accept the guiding principles of the team. In a scenario involving a team that has pride, a complete commitment to the purposes and values of the group has been made. This kind of pride is developed when leaders have a generous spirit that values all team members and always places others above themselves.

> *The good kind of pride is shared joy within the inner circle of teammates.*

The "good" kind of pride is not reserved for any elite group of individuals. It is available to any person or group who desires it and works toward the shared joy that is integral to it. Teams with this special, shared feeling develop loyalty, respect, and lifelong friendships and memories.

❑ **Great teams can *communicate*:**

> *"A teachable point of view, when combined with the proper teachable moment, makes for an optimum learning environment that can have a positive impact on the organization if you communicate quickly and at an instinctive level."*
> — Dr. Jim Peterson, author and philosopher

Great teams are characterized by a climate of trust based on good communication. It is much easier to support any teammate when you have a relationship based on open, honest, and direct communication. On the best of teams, communication (both positive and corrective) is appreciated and seen for what it really is—a statement that the coach cares for the athlete. Good communication allows every member of the team to feel secure in expressing his views and also facilitates a high degree of support for each other and the decisions of the group.

Correction should not be confused with criticism. Correction is a form of praise to an athlete where the coach is expressing the point that he believes that the athlete is capable of improving. When criticism is given, it is best to be done in a neutral tone and focused on the action, rather than the person or personality of the athlete. All criticism needs to be accompanied by a positive suggestion for individual or team improvement.

When individual team members can express themselves openly and confront mistakes and areas of confusion and frustrations, they will function much more effectively. Positive communication impacts the energy on a team. By confronting potential problems early and openly, these situations seldom get to the demoralizing stage of frustration and complaining. Team members must be willing to accept constructive correction, provide honest responses, and face issues head on.

Before problems arise, good teams revisit and review their designated goals and objectives on a regular basis. They agree on where they are going, why they need to get there, and assess how they are doing on the journey. When conflict does show itself, the team must return to its core values and realign itself with the purposes, goals, values, and mission statement as its main method for resolution. Mission statements need to be visible and adhered to every day, not only to help avoid or overcome adversity, but also to celebrate team successes.

Teams who have learned to communicate in a timely, professional manner say what they think, ask for help, share ideas, and are willing to risk making mistakes in front of each other. That attitude leads to consistent improvement, where the focus is on solutions. This situation only happens when leadership has created a trusting and caring atmosphere.

Communicating acceptance is critical for team-building and not difficult for coaches who use verbal cues as their primary method of reinforcement. Most players can live on a compliment for about a week, so give them at least one compliment a day to stay well ahead of their needs. Look for the good in each player and find the things that person is doing correctly, as often as you identify errors.

One positive area that can always be rewarded is physical effort. By clearly communicating to your players that their efforts to do their best for the team are important to you, regardless of the outcome of the play, a coach sends a message of acceptance to his athletes.

❑ **Great teams are *motivated*:**

> *"Every great achievement is the story of a flaming heart."*
> – Harry Truman

Within a motivated team itself, common agreement exists concerning expectations for the team. . . and those expectations are high. Great teams are able to start their own engine to excel, allowing their personal motivation to strengthen and build each other. The clearer the mission and focus are within the team, the easier it is to be motivated toward a united purpose. Teams will seldom exceed the shared expectations and level of motivation of the group.

On a motivated team, a strong *desire to succeed* exists among the team's leaders that is disseminated in a positive manner to everyone associated with the group. Motivated teams are competitive. Competition occurs for every position and for every role within the team. That competitive nature is appreciated by the best of teams and is often viewed as a means to improve the overall performance. Players tend to band together to utilize the energy that emanates from their competitive nature within the team against any opponent. They look forward to the toughest of competition and focus their preparation toward that vision. Prepare every practice for the best team you will play against. Motivation can come from within each person or from the outside. Teams are most effective when they are motivated by both sources.

> *"Leadership is the ability to lift and inspire."*
> — Paul Dietzel

As a point of fact, fear works as a motivator. In sport, as in life, either hope of a benefit or fear of a consequence triggers most motivation. Since most individuals coach as they were coached as players, if you grew up with coaches who used fear as the primary motivator, you probably began your coaching career with the same tactic. Fear works, but not nearly as well as love and respect. Love and respect bring a deeper purpose to your efforts to motivate others. Results of a team motivated through love and respect create great memories and lasting friendships. Tasks are completed, discipline accepted, and team and player expectations rise because teammates do not want to let each other down. They depend on and trust one another to complete their mission. Each role becomes equal in value to a team that values each other.

> *"The team is the star, never an individual player."*
> — John Wooden

Self-motivation is also essential for team success. The most successful leaders of teams have the ability to create conditions where the participants motivate and drive themselves. These leaders can make others see the best in themselves and build on those insights.

Teams that are made up of needy individuals, who require other people to get them going, do not tend to hold up in the long days of practice or the toughest of times during a season. They eventually crack or require so much attention that they get left behind. In reality, some sports exist that only attract self-directed participants. Athletes who require external motivation to work hard are not likely to survive in sports where success is based on a lot of solitary training that involves a lot of self-discipline and initiative (e.g., cross-country and swimming). If any athlete consistently depends on some other source for his motivation, he seldom will be able to sustain his level of motivation. Eventually, he can become an energy drag on the team.

Motivated teams work in an atmosphere of openness. They are not afraid to hustle, to try, to ask for help, or even to fail in front of each other. They are bound together by the same love and respect their leader has for them. Love of team, the sport, and competition helps bind them together.

One of the measuring sticks for the differences between teams is how long it takes and what it takes to stifle their motivation. Motivation can be curbed. A team that can go through failure or difficult times and maintain its high level of expectations and motivation will have a much greater chance of success than the group that gets discouraged at the first sign of a problem. Teams that have developed sincere friendship, camaraderie, and loyalty can withstand troubles much easier than groups that have not developed those types of relationships. This is often a reflection of leadership (both coaches and players).

Teams motivated by fear not only get discouraged more easily, but also can become resentful of the leader who is imposing the fear. On teams where fear has been used as the primary form of motivation and where punishment is given for mistakes, players will avoid taking on any responsibility to prevent making mistakes and receiving the anticipated punishment. Teams built around love, respect, and group responsibility tend to lean on each other in times of trouble and tend to be able to sustain their motivation for longer periods of time. Individually, they have learned to be an active participant in their own rescue, and collectively, they will not allow each other to get down.

> *"From a little spark may burst a mighty flame."*
> — Dante

❏ Great teams have *persistence*:

All factors being equal, adversity is a good thing for young people to experience. Winning all the time can mask problems and give young people an unrealistic view of life. Athletics is one of the best areas in a young person's life to enable an individual to experience the rigors of going through difficult times. Very few failures in athletics either do permanent damage or have lifelong implications. There is almost always another practice or game, and good teams have a built-in support system.

> *"The gem cannot be polished without friction, nor the person without trials."*
> — Unknown

No such thing as a perfect season, perfect game, or even a perfect practice session ever exists. Problems will always arise. Problems with winning and losing, injuries, relationships, etc. will emerge when they are least expected. Great teams can endure through the difficulties, which will occur during almost every athletic season. On great teams, when a problem exists, they solve it. All failures and problems need to be examined and dealt with directly. Methods should be devised that will prevent a problem from repeating itself. These teams also understand that it takes time to reach their potential individually and even longer collectively. They have no "quit" in them.

The ability of both teams and individuals to recover quickly from mistakes is one of the keys to success. Players who dwell on mistakes compound them. If your team has committed itself to continuous improvement, they must risk failure. Most games are just a series of mistakes, and it is the team that recovers the quickest from these mistakes that usually wins.

❑ Great teams have players who understand their *roles*:

"The strength of the wolf is in the pack and the strength of the pack is in the wolf."

— Rudyard Kipling

Great teams have individual players who each makes his own unique contribution to the group's success. At least one player needs to have the skills to perform each of the duties necessary for the team to collectively function. For example, every basketball team must have passers; every volleyball team must have a setter; etc. Although some roles appear to have more importance than others do, in reality, it is the combination of skills (roles) that allows a team to reach its ultimate potential. Roles give a player an identity. Every team member can bring a different skill to the total picture. Clarification and specification of roles aid in the acceptance and performance of those roles by each individual. It is essential that all the players understand their "shared" roles in order for the team to be effective. When each member understands his own role, as well as the roles of his teammates, he will be much more productive and feel more able to participate to the fullest. In the process, a "team identity" will begin to be formed.

When leadership gives each role equal value in the eyes of the team, everyone's role is more readily accepted and appreciated. Leadership will have difficulty building a team atmosphere if importance is placed on only a few "high-profile" roles. Consider basketball, for example. It is obvious to everyone who watches a game that the people who score are important and receive the most attention. But, if it were not for the player that made the pass to the scorer or the player who set the screen to free up the scorer, the team would not have succeeded in scoring. Basketball, like most sports, involves a number of equally valuable roles. Rebounders, defensive-stoppers, screeners, passers, decision-makers, encouragers, leaders, followers, perimeter-scorers, and interior-scorers must all fulfill their roles for the team to play as one unit.

When I coached basketball, I encouraged the attitude that scoring is a team effort by using a technique that involved how we had our players anticipate and answer questions after a game. The most commonly asked question after a game by people who are not focused on "team" is, "how many points did you get?" Our players were instructed to interpret "you" as "team." Rather, when they heard that question, they were asked to process the inquiry, "how many points did you (the team) score?" Whether they personally scored 25 or two points, they responded with the total number of points the team scored (e.g., 85). This exercise is a small example of focusing on the group effort and emphasizing the value that every role has in a team situation.

Roles can either be a force that binds the team together or creates jealousy between the individual parts. If value is shown equally to every role, it is easier for each role to be embraced by every player. The more each individual squad member feels like he is part of the team, the more he will likely contribute. The more each member contributes, the more he will feel like an integral part of the team and the team's overall success.

Statistics are another example of how roles can be emphasized and valued. If a basketball coach only keeps and displays statistics that indicate points and rebounds, that is what is being shown as having perceived value. If you give a successful screen and pass the same importance as the basket, you have just shown equal value. Keep track of and post the things that will really make you a good team. For example, if it is important for you to have players who dive on the floor for a loose ball, then keep a statistical category of how many times each player goes on the floor in an aggressive, purposeful manner.

Players tend to form an identity within the team for the positive role they fulfill. In turn, they will relish their role even more. Confidence derived from effectively performing a role within a team will allow that player to invest more energy for the benefit of the team. The power of an effective team is directly proportional to the effort each team member brings to his individual skills and role.

Just as roles must be established within the group of players, they must also be present for your coaching staff. All coaches must understand, accept, and fulfill the specific needs of the coaching team. Delegation of coaching responsibilities is essential, so each job is completed and not duplicated. The head coach must ensure that every job necessary for the success of the team is done well and is accorded perceived value.

> *"Organize, deputize, and supervise."*
> — Biff Jones

❑ **Great teams have a *positive attitude*:**

Attitude is a choice, but often one that has to be taught. Identify and define as specifically as possible what a positive attitude should be in your program. The clearer your description, the more likely your players will understand and be able to meet your standards. Teams are very much like any other relationship; they must be constantly worked at in order to function well.

> *"One of the illusions of life is that the present hour is not the critical, decisive hour. Write it on your heart that every day is the best day of the year."*
> — Ralph Waldo Emerson

As previously discussed, the definition I used for an athletic attitude when I coached involved the following: *"Be aggressive, disciplined, and love to compete. Be intelligent enough to listen and develop the self-motivation to work hard and learn. Have faith in the people you are working with and always put the team ahead of yourself. Keep your perspective and sense of humor."* As a coach, it then becomes important for you to define each area (aggressive, disciplined, loving to compete, etc.) so that all your team members and coaches are on the exact same page.

Having a positive athletic attitude can and should be used as one of your main criteria for squad selection. If you are able to establish a standard in attitude and use the period devoted to squad selection as the "line in the sand," it will help everyone involved on the team. For the player who needs to make changes, the coach should begin working with him long before the season begins and do everything in his power to assist that individual in making the necessary changes. That player will be helped by knowing well ahead of time exactly what is going to be accepted and what behaviors will not. There should not be any surprises for either party by the time tryouts begin. Once standards of behavior have been established and held to, the people who are sincerely interested in making your team will know and make the right choices. As such, the coach should have very few, if any, cuts based on attitude. Having an athletic attitude was my criteria for a player becoming part of the team. The players who do have a great athletic attitude deserve to have teammates who are as committed, disciplined, hardworking, and coachable as they are.

> *"Coaches have a tendency to stay too long with people with 'potential.' Try to avoid those players and go with a proven attitude. Players who live on 'potential' are coach killers. As soon as you find out who the coach killers are on your team, the better off you are. Go with the guys who have less talent but more dedication, more singleness of purpose."*
> – Don Shula

Successful coaches surround themselves with positive, energetic people who share their passion for life, sport, and team. Positive attitude is a choice every person can make on a daily basis. Keep in mind that everything is how you choose to see it.

Final Thoughts on Great Teams

Teams that have developed the right kind of pride and are motivated by love and respect tend to reflect an openness of value and persist through difficulties. Players on that type of team understand, accept, and embrace their roles, and maintain a positive attitude. When a person makes the decision to join in a team effort, the wisest choice he can make is to totally forsake any sense of self-interest and to commit his specialized skills to the building of the group.

Professional golf is one of the least likely team activities. Each player competes weekly as an "independent contractor," measuring success completely by his personal performance, alone against the field. As such, golfers are rewarded only for individual accomplishments. However, the impact of moving from independence to the interdependence of a team can be seen every time the Ryder Cup competition is held. The Ryder Cup is played every two years and includes a variety of team-format competitions that feature players from the United States against golfers from Europe. These same golfers who compete all year in a private, emotionless state are transformed into a team that depends on each other to determine a final outcome. Emotions run high. As a result, celebrations and disappointments are normally not held back. Players who play under pressure for huge amounts of money every week discover the magic and the added pressure of representing their country and being in a position where other players are depending on them for success. As 2002 team captain, Curtis Strange, described it, "Everything about the Ryder Cup is more pressure; it is more difficult than any major championship." While it is more difficult, it is also (in the players' own words), "more enjoyable than any other event," for one simple reason—the players are part of something bigger than themselves.

Another great example of the benefits of teamwork comes from the study of goose behavior. As a coach, you can learn the following team-building lessons from geese:

- *Team-first attitude*. As each bird flaps its wings, it creates uplift for the bird that is following it. By flying in a "V" formation, the whole flock adds 71 percent greater flying distance than if one bird was flying on its own. Lesson: When you share a common direction and rely on the strength of each other, you can get where you are going quicker and easier.

- *Roles*. Whenever a goose falls out of formation, it suddenly feels the air resistance of flying alone and quickly gets back into formation, so it can take advantage of the lifting power of the birds in front of him. Lesson: Be willing to accept the help of others, as well as do your part toward the task of the team.

- *Positive attitude*. The geese in the back of the formation continually honk to encourage those up in front who are having to work harder to keep their speed. Lesson: Recognize and encourage those team members who need it the most. Positive encouragement is much stronger than any other form of reinforcement. Positive attitude is a choice that each individual can make to help the team reach its potential.

- *Perseverance and loyalty*. When a goose gets sick or wounded, two other geese from the formation follow it down to the ground to help and protect it. They remain with their partner until the goose either can fly or dies. Then, they begin their trip again, by either catching up with their group or joining another formation. Lesson: Great teammates stand by each other in times of trouble.

Hopefully every person involved in athletics at any level will get the opportunity to experience being on a *great team* at least once during his life. Teams provide coaches with unforgettable moments, and help define the purpose of those who coach. On a team where all participants are aligned toward a common, clearly defined goal and are willing to tackle challenging tasks, a lot can be accomplished. With a sense of friendship and loyalty to each other, plus a personal responsibility for the outcome, a positive, productive atmosphere can be established.

Great teams are made up of individual athletes who have consciously given up their quest for personal glory, who have willingly and wholeheartedly embraced the character traits of a team player, and who have fully committed themselves to the group effort. Collectively, this attitude is one of the coach's greatest legacies.

CHAPTER 10

Team Building Through Positive Conditioning

> *"The coach's most powerful tool is love."*
>
> – John Wooden

Coaching, when done correctly, can have lasting value in a young person's life, regardless of the player's skill level or success. This chapter is designed to make you think and reassess how you build a team feeling and also how you view conditioning.

Although you may not agree with every point made in this chapter, you need to keep in mind that the concept of positive conditioning really is effective. It consistently works with either gender or any sport where additional conditioning is a requirement for team success.

If coaches had a choice of being thought of as "positive" or "negative," the vast majority of individuals in this profession would undoubtedly choose "positive." Most coaches believe that being positive gets better results. Without question, being positive is the best approach to reinforcement and coaching.

> *"You can motivate players better with a kind word than you can with a whip."*
>
> – Bud Wilkinson
>
> *"Coaching is a profession of love – you can't coach people unless you love them."*
>
> – Eddie Robinson

Many methods exist for developing team feeling—some are contrived, while others are sincere and believable. The following method is a proven method for bringing teams together in a sincere, believable way. It also is a method to turn what some coaches consider to be the "worst," or at least the most negative, part of practice (conditioning) into one of the best. I believe it is a positive change both for the coaches and for the players.

Early and throughout my coaching career, I went to watch other coaches work. It offered one of the best opportunities to improve professionally. As such, coaches are encouraged to identify who the best coaches are in their area and go observe them in practice. What sport or age they coach is not as important as their ability to teach. You will discover as I did that there are all types of coaches. One of the unique features of the coaching profession is that it allows for so much autonomy. You will find that there are as many different successful styles as there are different personalities.

One of the primary reasons that I visited so many schools was an attempt to see for myself why certain coaches are "great." Why are they able to consistently field competitive teams? Why do their players love them? How do they consistently get their teams' best effort? How do they demand and receive appropriate behavior?

Among the factors that I observed and learned from my visits were:

- Go observe practice sessions. Don't evaluate a coach by watching his teams play a game. It is too easy to get caught up in comparison of athletes or the outcome of the game.

- Try to attend practices on a series of days. While you may see many things in the first few minutes, watch for a few days and many other lessons will become apparent. Don't make judgments based on one practice.

- Go observe a different program for a week every year.

- Watch and listen closely to see how the coaches you observe go about building their teams.

- Watch and listen to see how these coaches interact and develop relationships with their players. Relationships are the most critical part of a coach's job.

- Observe how athletes react to their coaches in times of praise and in times of correction.

The following examples illustrate some of the best techniques that I learned during my coaching career about building a team (from both personal experience and observation):

- You build a good team when good leadership exists. The leadership of the coach determines everything. In every instance where there was great leadership, there was a good team.

- You build a good team when coaches understand how to achieve a balanced combination of fun and discipline. All "fun" is generally unproductive time, while all "discipline" is not much different than forced labor.

- You build a team when the group attains tough goals, faces tough challenges together, and has common bonds. That is how team toughness and determination are formed. The best way to describe coaches who can consistently reach this level is someone who is both positive and demanding. A *positive-demanding coach* gets teams to work hard and set and reach attainable goals. He also finds a way to get his players to enjoy the experience.

- You build good teams when mutual respect exists between players and coach. A feeling of interdependence exists within the group, an attitude that the team is more important than any individual. These coaches usually rely on their own discretion and are not boxed in by too many rules. Rules can get in the way of effective leadership.

Conditioning

When observing other coaches, I saw many successful methods of building teams, each of which helped me formulate my coaching philosophy. On the other hand, I still struggled with how I was doing the conditioning phase of practice.

When you think back to your own memories of conditioning as an athlete, what do you recall? Examples of the types of responses that coaches commonly offer with regard to this question include:

- "It was hard, difficult, unpleasant."

- "We ran when someone on the team fouled up" (we all paid).

- "We ran more if someone didn't finish in a certain time."

- "We ran when the coach was mad."

- "We remember hating the coach."

- "Trying to avoid killing yourself."

- "As long as I wasn't last, I wouldn't be noticed."

- "We ran harder if it was measured or when we were being watched."

- "We remembered that certain days of the week were always hard conditioning days and we tried to coast through practice to have something left."

None of these memories reflect an approach that is either pleasant or beneficial for building a team. In my coaching career, I learned the following about conditioning from observing other coaches (some good, some bad):

- A lot of "positive coaches" go easy on the conditioning because they don't want to be an "ogre" to their players. Therefore, their teams don't do as much conditioning as necessary and are not in as good of shape as some of their opponents.

- As much as possible, well-organized coaches achieve their conditioning goals by the pace of their practices.

- One effective method of conditioning involves breaking up the conditioning periods throughout practice, instead of doing it all at the end of the practice session.

- Fear works as a motivator. Fear will get players to run hard. Fear will capture their attention for short periods of time. *On the other hand, while fear works, it does not work nearly as well as motivating through love and respect.*

- Most individuals coach as they were coached. Whatever methods were used with coaches as players is how they at least begin to form their own coaching style.

Regardless of all the people I watched and all the things I tried, the way I was handling conditioning still didn't reflect who I was or wanted to be as a coach. I couldn't reduce my expectations for the level of condition I felt my teams needed to be in to compete at their best. By the same token, I often found myself having to build up some sense of anger or find mistakes and using them as reasons why I was going to run the players hard.

I spent a lot of time trying to find the style that would fit my philosophy and still accomplish the level of conditioning that I felt my teams required to be successful. The "smart" side of me said the goal should be to take things that were important to me and essential for team success (conditioning) and find a way to make them equally important to the players.

The "positive" side of me said that I had to find a way to take things that are not inherently fun and make them enjoyable. Conditioning and coaching should not be "forced labor" or motivated through fear. In my mind, the choice was clear – I had to shift my thinking.

In this regard, I wanted to achieve the following objectives:

- To be in better game condition than any of our opponents
- To have our condition be a source of pride
- To not have to be upset to get them to run

As such, this is what I believed to be true:

- Being good is a privilege. Having fun for an athlete involves being good.
- The greatest management principle of motivation refers to the fact that *things*

that get rewarded get done, and those things will perpetuate themselves. This precept is especially true if you are rewarding "student-owned behaviors," or choices. Effort is a "student-owned" behavior that is completely within the athlete's control.

- If you reward an OK effort and call it "great," you'll get an OK effort. If you reward a good effort as great, you will get a good effort. On the other hand, if you only reward *great* effort, you will get *great* effort, and the great effort will perpetuate itself. Accordingly, if you only reward what you consider "great" or improved effort until it becomes great, then your players will be more likely to reach the desired level. You can always say "that was better," for an improved effort. But do not say "that was great," if it wasn't.

- The best form of reinforcement is positive. The best forms of positive reinforcements are verbal, physical, and love.

My goal then became to take what I *knew* and get what I *wanted*. Subsequently, I used the following steps to change the way my players looked at conditioning. I introduced the theory by verbally asking them if they believed the following premises (which, in turn, led to the listed conclusion):

Premise #1. Being in great condition will make you a better player. True or false? Being a better individual player will make us a better team. True or false?

Premise #2. Conditioning will allow us to have more success. True or false? Conditioning is something the best teams at any level always have. True or false?

Conclusion: Therefore, conditioning should be looked at as a privilege. True or false?

Once they accepted the aforementioned conclusion, I was able to adapt the following ideas:

- The better practice they had, the more conditioning I would provide for them.

- Effort = praise. Since great work habits are developed from praising *effort*, the coaches praised all *great* effort, regardless of time or outcome.

- If you won a competition, you were *allowed* to run, and if you lost, you did not *get* to run.

- As coaches, we had to learn to reward our best workers, instead of getting upset at the poor workers. We also had to stop punishing those players who were trying their best, but happened to have been born with an unacceptable level of foot speed, by making them or the whole team run again when they finished last or with a slower-than-established time. The immediate result was that more of these foot-slow players became good workers. If we had some players who continued to give a poor effort, we had made a mistake in squad selection, and they had to be eliminated if they could not (or would not) change their work habits. Giving less than your best effort is a selfish, player-owned decision.

- By positively recognizing and reinforcing great effort, we consistently got great effort. Once you are getting your athletes' best effort, there will be a natural skill progression and an increased level of conditioning.

Positive Conditioning

All factors considered, the actual techniques used to condition your players are not as important as the consistency and reinforcement you employ to motivate your athletes toward their best efforts. Many coaches feel like they must constantly create different conditioning drills to keep their athletes from being bored. On the other hand, we found that we were able to carry over many of the same running sequences that we had used before and just add the new reinforcement techniques. Think of the drills you currently use to condition your team and whether they have provided a sufficient fitness level. See if you can adjust the reinforcement techniques you employ and use the same drills.

No matter what drills we employed for conditioning, the developmental focus of most of these exercises concentrated on cardiovascular fitness (i.e., stamina, aerobic fitness). We then designed the drills around the criteria that we used for building teams, including:

- Depending on each other
- Achieving tough, common goals
- Balancing fun and discipline
- Relying on mutual respect by providing dignity
- Being positive but demanding in our leadership
- Encouraging athletes to abide by one single rule – "don't let your teammates down"

Employing Positive Conditioning

Every coach should verbally reinforce great efforts that occur in any of the conditioning activities. One of the most important aspects of positive conditioning is to provide an opportunity for dignity. For example, allow players to take off extra clothing (in football, having the players take their helmets off allows the coaches to see effort on the faces of each player). Yes, they play with their helmets on, but wouldn't you rather see their faces and have them be able to hear your praise? Allow time for players to recover from the previous conditioning effort particularly if it was rigorous or intense (e.g., sprinting), so they can give their best effort. One of the techniques that can be used to ensure that all of your players are able to recover and be ready and willing to give full effort is to have them individually raise their hands when they are prepared for the next conditioning activity. This step allows each player to recover at his own rate. By putting his hand up, it also says, "I commit to full effort."

If you have players who want to excuse themselves from conditioning because they are not feeling well (or for any other reason), let them out. Do not force them to exercise. Conditioning should be a privilege. Do not let them stand there and watch the others engage in the conditioning activities. Rather, have them go in while you give the players who are present full praise for their effort.

"Don't let your teammates down" was the only rule we had for our teams. During conditioning, that rule provides a different incentive for individual players to exercise. Beyond conditioning, that single rule encompasses all areas of athletic behavior and leaves you a wide amount of discretion. It covers such aspects as effort, attention, punctuality, academic progress, and decisions on weekends. "Don't let your teammates down" is a way of reinforcing the fact that the team is relying on each individual to make good choices and that the team is always more important than any individual player.

Conditioning Drills

The following conditioning drills can be performed to meet the developmental needs of your athletes:

- *Timed Running Drill*

This drill involves setting a goal to have your players run for a certain amount of time (based upon distance and number of players). During this running, watch for every opportunity to verbally reward effort, but also to identify if any player is not giving an appropriate effort. If you see poor or marginal effort, you should stop the running drill for the entire team. Without publicly singling out who the offender was, the team needs to know that unless every player is committed to an all-out effort, the drill will not continue. Usually, all you have to say is that "at least one player was not giving his best, and the team needs the best effort of EVERY player." "We are depending on you, don't let your teammates down and tomorrow will be another chance to have everyone give their best." All factors considered, the better they want to be as a team, the more it will bother them to be stopped, and the longer they will want to set their time goals. If the point in the conditioning drill where they had to be stopped occurs in the middle of practice, you should just go on to the next section of practice. If it happens at the end of practice, you should declare that practice is done for the day, with the understanding that tomorrows' practice could be better and they would have another opportunity to enhance their level of conditioning at that time.

Similar to cardiovascular exercises, you can employ the same principles to perform strengthening exercises as well. If you tell your players to "do 30 push-ups," there may be some athletes, who no matter how hard they try, can not do 30. On the other hand, there may be some players who are capable of doing many more than 30. For these players, doing 30 push-ups is not even a challenge. But, if you say, "see how many push-ups you can do in 30 seconds," that allows the player who can only do 15 to give his maximum effort and be straining for number 16 at the end of the designated time and be receiving praise for his effort. It also allows the player who is capable of doing 45 push-ups in 30 seconds to demonstrate all the push-ups he is capable of doing, and receive praise for his effort, not his ability to do just 30 push-ups.

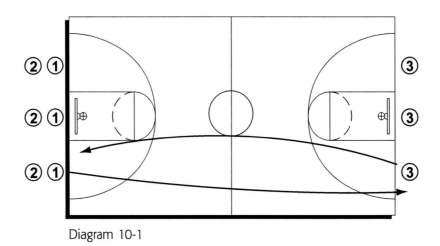

Diagram 10-1

• *Three-Person Exchange Drill*

This drill involves timed running. Most timed running is done using interval training (three- or four-person exchange). In this drill, players line up in groups of three or four, depending on how much rest you want them to have between sprints. If you have an odd number of players and have one line with four individuals, when you want everyone running in groups of three, just combine two players and have them run at the same time (bottom group). In Diagram 10-1, players #1 and #2 remain at one end of the distance (e.g., 30 to 100 yards in sports such as football and soccer or a court-length in sports such as basketball and volleyball), while #3 is positioned on the opposite end of the designated area. In this drill, #1 runs to #3 and stays at that end; #3 runs and tags #2 and stays there; and #2 runs and exchanges with #1. Each player goes through the pattern of run-rest, and run-rest until the designated period of time has expired.

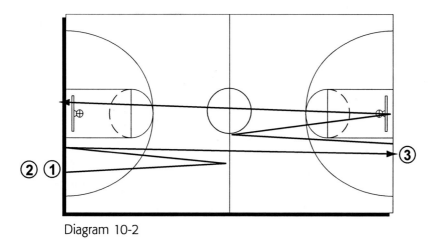

Diagram 10-2

• *Half-Court, Back, Full-Court Drill*

This drill is the same type of exercise as the previous exercise, only it employs change-of-direction running. In Diagram 10-2, players #1 and #2 line up on the starting line, while player #3 lines up at the opposite end of the area involved. This drill can be done on a basketball court (as shown in Diagram 10-2) or on a field with the distances varied. The first player in each line starts and goes to the half-court line, reverses his direction and sprints back to the place he started, and then reverses his direction again and sprints to the far end to player #3. Player #1 tags #3 and stays there, as #3 goes half-court and back and then full-court to exchange with #2. Players see how many full-effort sprints they can get in during the allotted time.

• *Individual Maximum Efforts Drill*

This drill may be as simple as determining how many sprints each individual player can do during a specific time period. After sprinting, each player should rest so he can go all-out on his next effort. Players will be running the same distances, but at different times, and not on a command. The coach must establish distances and times that are challenging, but possible, and are appropriate to the needs of their sport. Players should challenge themselves to do as many quality-effort sprints as possible in the allotted time. Coaches need to focus on praising the maximum efforts of players who are running, and not get sidetracked by players who are resting. If you are reinforcing correctly, players will normally do everything in their power to hear *their name* as many times as possible during this time.

If you decide to run this type of conditioning, you should begin this section of your practice by allowing your athletes to set the length of running time for that day. It is wise to discuss with team leaders the value of gradually increasing the time and number of sprints that the team should be required to do with maximum efforts. This style of running allows each player to work to his maximum capacity, depending on how quickly he can recover individually. Vary the recovery times, so that your stronger players get an opportunity for more sprints and your less-conditioned players will still be able to receive praise for the efforts they are able to give. Each player should strive to achieve his personal best and not compare with his teammates. Conducting this drill in this way enables all players to benefit by improving their level of physical condition.

- *Run for Certain Number of Sprints Drill*

This drill involves having the team leadership set a goal for the number of untimed sprints they want the team to run on a specific day. Again, you should allow recovery time, praise every great effort, and stop the group if you have anyone who is not putting forth his best effort. It is wise to meet with your team leaders throughout the season and talk about how to set realistic goals, and how and when to increase the number of sprints they are attempting. While this drill is tougher on those players who are not as well-conditioned, adequate recovery time enables them to wait until they are completely ready to run again.

- *Run After Being Successful or Winning Drill*

This drill involves the unique stipulation that "winners run." One of the biggest psychological changes in this form of reinforcement is the thought of "winners run." Usually, winning prevents players from "having" to run. This drill takes the opposite tact. If you are unsuccessful, you do not get to run. One example of a specific drill where success allows running in basketball is "one-and-one and run." In this drill, if you are interspersing the conditioning throughout practice, and your players are going to shoot free throws for three or four minutes, you would have each player shoot a one-and-one. If a player misses either shot, he gets back in his shooting line. If he makes both attempts of the one-and-one, he *gets* to run down and back.

- *Help Your Buddy Drill*

In this drill, individuals get into lines of three or four players at the starting point. On the starting command, the first player in each line (#1) runs the required distance and returns to the starting point. The next player (#2) in line watches his "buddy" who is running. He has the option of stepping in and running for him when he returns to the starting point. You should encourage player #2 to watch the running form, speed, and face on his teammate (#1) who is running. If he is straining, losing form, or struggling to maintain his speed, #2 can raise his hand, offer help ("I've got you buddy"), and decide when to step in. Player #1 must stop and allow #2 to take his place. It is entirely the decision of #2. Player #2 then begins running his sprints. At this point, player #3 has the decision on when to replace #2.

This drill promotes several factors that can help improve conditioning and also build team feeling. The runners should attempt to run as long as possible, without slowing or straining so they will not be replaced. The person waiting should be looking for an opportunity to assist a teammate in trouble. The idea of "helping your buddy" or "not letting your buddy down" is contagious – an attitude that likely will be carried over into other areas of practice and games.

- *Ask for Help Drill*

This drill is set up exactly the same way as the previous conditioning drill. This time, the first player in each line starts running the set distance on the signal and goes as long as he can without stopping, while giving maximum effort. It is the runner's call for help that allows the next runner to enter the sprint. Unless he asks for help, the next runner must stay and wait his turn. The concept of being able to push yourself and be your own judge on how long you can go is a natural motivator. The idea of trying to increase the number of consecutive sprints you can make before needing help will improve the conditioning level of each individual who pushes himself. The situation of running in a "spotlight" makes it difficult for any player to give less than his best effort.

The concept of being willing to "ask for help" is essential within successful teams. It is OK to say, "I need help, will you step in for me." Frequently, the most difficult aspect of the drill will be to get the runner to surrender. He will try to go too far. This is a dramatic change from an athlete's traditional mentality towards conditioning.

- *Weakest Link in the Chain Drill*

When the weakest link in the chain drill is employed, it can be done in small groups or large groups. The most effective approach is to have the entire team attempt to reach a specified goal. One example of how this drill could be conducted would be to have all of the team members line up across the starting position. You would then have them interlock elbows or hold hands to create a chain. The running goal is then set, and the team all begins running together on the command. The goal for the team is to reach the running objective without ever breaking the chain (i.e., the weakest link). An example of a possible running goal for football, for example, may be:

- Runners start at the goal line with their hands linked.

- Run to the 10-yard line and stop.

- Turn around, reconnect hands, and, on the command, sprint back to the original start line without breaking the chain.

- Recover, sprint to the 20, turn, and, on command, sprint back.

- Repeat the drill until everyone has run 50 or even 100 yards.

In this scenario, for example, your players will learn early that if they have two slower, heavier runners together, these two "hefty" individuals would often get so far behind that the chain would break. Rather than look toward them as the reason for failure, the stronger, faster players will quickly learn that to prevent the chain from breaking, they must stand on either side of the slower runners and help them along without breaking the link. Again you are not only conditioning your team, while achieving a tough goal, you are also creating a mindset where a more conditioned player wants to help a teammate succeed or assist a teammate who wants to have the whole team accomplish their desired goal.

- *Run With Other Teams Drill*

If you have another team during your season that is also using the principles of positive conditioning, it can provide additional motivation to combine both programs in the same conditioning drills. Since you are looking for and praising effort, the speed or strength of the participants can be completely different. For example, you can conduct a drill where both genders are combined in sports such as basketball, football, and softball or even where high school athletes are grouped with members of youth teams. In this situation, it is fun for both groups to cheer for each other. Furthermore, they gain an appreciation for the efforts of classmates, regardless of the age, sport, or speed. You can intermix the groups in three- or four-person exchanges. In the process, you can develop a positive attitude and a heightened level of conditioning for your own team, as well as build respect for the efforts of the other team (i.e., program pride and support).

- *Winner's Circle Drill*

This drill involves a scenario where you set tough, but achievable, goals, so that your team can all end practice in the "winner's circle." Set a goal for each group of runners, so that the stronger runners can help teammates who are not as well-conditioned. Once a particular group has reached its individual goal, the members of the group all go into an area designated as the "winner's circle." The basic objective of the drill is to have the entire team accomplish a set goal and all end up in the circle before time expires. This drill could be conducted in a variety of ways and settings. For example, a group of three basketball players could be required to run a full-speed, half-court, back, full-court sprint and then make both ends of a one-and-one free throw. In football, a group of three or four players could be required to run cross-field sprints, with all players running at the same time. Each group would attempt to run the same set number of sprints in the allotted amount of time. As soon as your group completes the set number, move to the winner's circle and encourage the remaining groups. Occasionally, you can allow those players who finish early to go contribute to a team that has not reached its goal yet. They would then combine their group total to try to reach a set number. Again, you have a group of players working together to achieve a goal, with teammates and coaches encouraging or offering help. Coaches or group leaders should balance the teams to give each group a reasonable opportunity to succeed.

- *Eliminator Drill*

In traditional conditioning practices, the first several players who finish are done and are allowed to go into the locker room, while all of the other players are forced to go back and run another sprint. This procedure usually continues until only the slowest runners are left.

The other method that is often used to conduct this drill involves a scenario where if the whole team doesn't finish under a certain time, then the whole team runs again. This method does nothing to promote team unity, and usually results in faster players being upset at their teammates, who just happen to not be gifted with speed and therefore cause the group to have to run again (i.e., forced labor, based upon outcome, not effort). The faster players can coast and still make the required time. On the other hand, the slower players may be giving everything they have and still have no chance to finish under the time limit, regardless of how much they try.

The eliminator drill can be conducted in a manner similar to the "winner's run" drill, where the players who finish last in a race are "eliminated" from further running, while the fastest runners can continue to condition.

One of the most powerful drills at your disposal is the eliminator. Coaches can choose any sprint distance they want (e.g., 40-yard sprint, crosscourt 16's, half-court, full-court), as long as the distance is equal for all competitors. You should use this drill sparingly (i.e., two or three times per season). You should only use this drill if the whole team has bought in to your conditioning program. On the day that this drill is performed, you should have already done other conditioning exercises. For the first time in the conditioning process, players are eliminated, based upon their speed.

In football, for example, all of the players would begin on the goal line, with the finish line 40 yards away. On the start signal, all players sprint for the finish line. Coaches praise all of the maximum efforts, but watch to see who the last five players across the line are. Those five are eliminated but do not leave the field. Instead, they join the coaches as encouragers for the players remaining in the drill. The players left in the drill then jog back to the goal line and recover at their own rate. Each athlete commits to maximum effort when he has recovered by raising his hand. Once all hands are raised, the coach gives the signal to start the next sprint. Again, the last five finishers are eliminated and join the group of encouragers. The remaining players repeat the process of jogging back and recovering. Coaches eliminate players – five at a time – until the group reaches a total of 10 players. At that point, the coaches reduce the participants two at a time, until they reach the final four. When the group is reduced to only four players, the coaches then eliminate one player at a time. The other players are employed to form a tunnel for the final players to sprint through. At the conclusion of each sprint, the remaining players in the drill are allowed as much time as necessary to recover before being required to sprint again. The players who have been eliminated are commended by everyone if they have given their best effort. By the time you get to the final two, the fastest players have run quite a few competitive sprints. After the final two have run against each other, you can then give the winner the option of running one by himself after he has recovered. Most players in this situation usually choose to run one sprint alone.

Players often dive for the line to try to keep from being one of the last five or to get to the next round. We once had the two final players both simultaneously dive for the line to have the privilege of running one sprint by themselves. Occasionally, the final player, running by himself, will dive across the finish line as the tunnel of teammates cheers him through the 40 yards.

• *Push Day*

A "push day" can be scheduled once you completely believe that your team has bought in to the positive-conditioning concept and is doing everything in their power to push themselves and help each other. In other words, they have become a great team. For teams that reach this level, coaches can decide to schedule a "push day" (usually, only on a once-a-year basis). In this drill, you go through a normal practice, followed by the most strenuous conditioning session of the year. At the conclusion of the conditioning, you bring your players together and talk about how much of conditioning is mental and how they are capable of so much more than they think or have ever done. When they think they have just completed the most difficult conditioning of their life, you then ask them if they believe they are capable of more. Then you start over and repeat the entire conditioning section, doubling the most strenuous day of the year. When I was coaching, it was a tradition for our teams to anticipate and look forward to being challenged, knowing that the coaches must really think they are a special team to qualify for a "push day." Most teams will look back on that day as a standard for not quitting, for achieving a goal that they did not believe was possible, and as a unifying moment. It is something they are proud to have accomplished. It becomes part of who they are as a team and as an individual athlete. It is something that they will remember long after all the games are finished. In my personal experience, athletes from 20 years ago still say, "coach, I will never forget push day – that was physically the hardest day of my life, but it is a great memory."

Summary Points

Utilize your imagination and creativity to develop drills that serve your conditioning purposes, and then employ the motivation principles of rewarding effort. You can use almost any conditioning drill, just change the focus of the verbal reinforcement from *outcome* to *effort*.

The results will speak for themselves. Your most talented athletes will have a chance to be both your best workers and the best conditioned. This situation is what you need if you are going to rely on them to carry the physical load for the team. Possibly even more importantly, because they get their efforts praised, this approach to conditioning will enable your weaker athletes to be in better condition and to be able to feel good about themselves and their contribution to the team. Your bigger or slower players will love the concept of rewarding effort and will enjoy being part of this system of reinforcement. As such, they will hate to be cut out of the "eliminator," and want to continue running.

One of the key elements in the success of the positive conditioning concept is that once your team has completely bought in to this philosophy, you should give them ownership. Rather than viewing the situation as, "look what I have done as a coach," the player-oriented focus is on, "look at who you have become." The players are the ones doing the work, while trying not to let their teammates down. They are the ones who look at conditioning as a privilege and see the benefits of being part of an unselfish unit.

You will find with teams that have made a conscious choice to buy in to this concept that the worst punishment you can give them is to not allow them to run. As such, if you have a practice where there is poor effort or poor concentration, you simply do not allow the team to condition. Just like positive effort and behavior, poor effort or concentration are "student-owned" choices.

This conditioning concept also requires a complete buy-in from your entire coaching staff, not just you, as the head coach. Once you have gone in this direction, you can not revert back to previous methods and philosophies of conditioning your team. One instance of getting upset during practice and saying to your team, "that was bad, get on the line, and you are going to run" will cause you and your system to lose credibility.

If you are able to make the transition from a traditional approach to conditioning to a positive-conditioning philosophy, the following will be true:

- You will not believe how hard your players will work

- You will not believe how they support and encourage each other

- You will not believe how much closer they become when they are pulling for each other instead of having to run as punishment for mistakes or outcome

- You will not believe how much harder you are able to push your team

- You will not believe how much better they feel about themselves and their team as they leave the practice area

- You will not believe how much different you feel as an encourager, rather than a slave driver

In a profession that has lasting value to life, recall the previous discussion concerning the point that most individuals coach as they were coached. In turn, if you are able to make this one change, consider what you are doing for the *next generation of coaches*, as well as for helping to create positive memories for your current athletes.

PART IV

Focusing on Other Issues

"A child's life is like a piece of paper on which every passerby leaves a mark."

— Chinese proverb

CHAPTER 11

Transitioning Athletes Within a Program

One of the "hot topics" in the educational community these days is transitioning students from one grade to the next, one school to the next, or one level of subject matter (e.g., math, science, etc.) to the next. Much of the success of individual students is dependent on the teachers being involved and working with the students to help coordinate and facilitate their movement to the next "level."

Athletic transitioning is no different. It requires cooperation and organization to move the athletes from one level of competition to the next with as little disruption of learning as possible. When done correctly, it is much like smoothly passing a baton in a relay race. The "receiving" coach and the "giving" coach can either work together for the betterment of the student-athlete or be more concerned about themselves and their own program at the expense of the athletes. In this regard, any coach in the position of passing athletes to another coach could be considered a "feeder" coach.

This chapter has two separate areas of focus: 1) What the high school coach can do to help the feeder school coach; and 2) What the feeder school coach can do to help the high school coach.

What the High School Coach Can Do to Help the Feeder School Coach

The wise high school coach does not operate in isolation. The more you can provide teaching continuity within your program, the better it is for the athletes, and the easier it will be for them to move from one stage of your program to the next. As a rule, cooperation between coaches is a two-way street, but the high school coach has most of the responsibility for initiating the process. In order to share kids between coaches, you must be willing to share yourself, the credit, ideas, knowledge, and time. You must also support the feeder coaches, just as you would like them to support you. In this regard, the following factors apply:

- Your first responsibility is to be the individual who makes the initial attempt to build an alliance. Make the feeder coaches your ally. If friendship is not possible, at least develop a mutual respect based upon your mutual interest in working with kids.

- Acknowledge the value of what the feeder coaches have done to prepare the kids with whom you are now working. Too many coaches have a "they didn't know anything until I got hold of them" mentality. All the time and energy spent by these coaches was an unselfish gift. In fact, most coaches can recount numerous things that they did for the young people they coached.

- Offer time to share knowledge and terminology, and go through techniques. Take the time to go through all the breakdown drills you use to teach the essential skills of your sport.

- Offer opportunities for the feeder coaches to keep in contact with those athletes of yours that they had previously coached. One of the greatest things about coaching kids at a younger age is that you get a chance to be part of their lives for a longer period of time. Such an opportunity may be as simple as inviting the feeder coaches to your team's practices and games. Your locker room should always be open to them. You can also involve them in your coaching efforts or allow them to assist in the summer-league program (e.g., help coach a team). You should always make them feel welcome at post-game meetings or camps.

- Include the feeder coaches in the big picture, as part of the "whole program," and part of the "whole staff," by involving them in such activities as scouting, game planning, and end-of-the-year banquets. One of the best ways to connect with your feeder coaches is to take them as part of your staff when you attend coaching clinics.

- As the head high school coach, you can really help make a connection with the younger athletes by coming and watching them play games, or even more importantly, coming and watching them practice. Just your presence at practice can show them the importance you place on preparation.

- Find a method to get the younger players to attend your games. For example, you could establish a special pass or place and time for them to get into the games that is just for them. Being able to attend one pre-game or post-game meeting during the season can be a strong memory for a young athlete.

- Provide time for the older players to be around the younger ones on the court or the field to develop a "big brother – little brother" feeling. The fact that one of the high school players even knows his name can be a huge lift for a 10-year-old. Whenever possible, have your varsity athletes work with the younger players in a coaching situation.

- As an experienced coach, there are many things that you can do to help beginning coaches in your program. Above all, do not set them up for failure by leaving them stranded. With regards to assisting beginner coaches, the following examples illustrate steps that you can take:

  ✓ Develop a coaching *library of books and videos* that is available to them.

  ✓ Help them with *time management*. Most beginning coaches overestimate how much they can get done in a limited amount of time. Provide them with a checklist of essential and non-essential individual and team skills.

  ✓ Help with *practice planning* to allow their time to be expended as purposefully as possible, especially the time allotted to individual teaching time versus team concepts.

  ✓ Work with them on "classroom management" in the gym or on the field. Assist them with their efforts to *balance discipline and fun*, as well as how to establish rules and expectations that are reasonable and to which athletes can be held.

  ✓ Take the time to teach them how to break down and *teach a physical skill*, using the model, shape, and positive reinforcement method.

  ✓ Prepare them for the day when they must deal with angry or pushy *parents*, and be ready to come to their aid as the head of the program.

What the Feeder School Coach Can Do to Help the High School Coach

The feeder coaches must realize the importance of their job, as it fits into the big picture. They are a critical piece in the puzzle, and their main concern should be to make it easier for their athletes to move and succeed within the program. Even though these feeder coaches may be the "head coach" at their level, they need to be able to look beyond the time that they spend with each individual and team and visualize the finished product. There may be many times when they may not agree with style of play or technique taught by the head of the program, but their responsibility is to make the transitioning of their kids as easy as possible. Therefore, they must put themselves in a servant-leadership position.

As a feeder coach, whether you like or dislike the head of the program and his ideas, it is your responsibility to discuss these differences in private with the people involved and then provide a united front in public. The kids do not care about coaches' egos; they care about getting better and playing at the next level. As the feeder coach you must be willing to meet and try to build an allegiance with the head of the program. In athletics, the kids' needs come first.

With regard to specific steps that you can take to help the high school coach, consider the following:

- Two theories exist about how you should choose an offensive or defensive system. The first is to run the exact style as the high school. The second is to run your "own stuff." The correct answer for the feeder coach is to *do whatever the high school coach would like you to do*. That is what will allow your kids to make a good transition to the next team.

- Possibly more important than using the high school coach's entire offensive or defensive system is to *use the same terminology and technique*. Coaches who share terminology avoid forcing their athletes to learn a new language every time they change levels. Who cares whether you call something a "lead step" or an "open step." The only factor that matters is that the kids understand the term and skill. These are the times that you have to put your ego in your pocket and give your kids the best chance possible to succeed at the next level.

- Build a wide talent base. Not only do you have the responsibility to not run kids off, you need to try to *develop an interest and love of the game* in as many players as possible.

- Work hard to have each of your teams experience some success, and when they do, *teach them to attribute the success to the preparation* that they made. One of the most desirable contributions you can make for a high school program is to teach players how to prepare and then to make the connection between preparation and achievement. One of the worst things that can happen in younger athletes is for you to allow your players to think that they know all there is to know, and they are as good as they ever need to be. It is critical that players understand that they are capable of and responsible for getting better.

- *Define and develop an "athletic attitude" within your program* that establishes and holds athletes to positive behavioral expectations. Attitudes are easier to change at an early age. For every player you let slide with regard to tolerating unacceptable behavior, you are pushing that responsibility on to the next coach. It is important to hold all of your athletes to the same standards for behavior. It is essential that highly skilled athletes are held accountable for appropriate athletic behavior. Their infractions should not be excused or ignored because of their physical abilities. *Demand proper individual and team behavior* during all practices and games. Outstanding attention, effort, and sportsmanship are all choices that every athlete is capable of making.

- Teach your athletes at an early age how to accept *correction as a compliment*. Athletes who do not ever develop this attitude either feel that they are too self-important to admit that they do not already know everything, often take correction as personal criticism, or usually respond to correction with an excuse. None of these responses help the athlete in the future or with the next coach.

- *Focus on individual skills, but always within the team concept.* Working on individual skills will allow each athlete to progress at his own rate. But if young athletes do not learn how to operate within a team structure, they are missing one of the best lessons athletics can teach. Players who put their own skills above the importance of the team end up being selfish, egotistical performers who find it more important that they "win" than that the team "wins." All players need to learn how to put the team ahead of themselves.

- Help both the athletes and their parents *understand how the competitive pyramid narrows* as they move up in grade level. For example, they need to realize that of the more than three dozen girls who may be playing volleyball in seventh grade, somewhere between 3 to 10 of those individuals will still be playing by the time they are seniors. As such, one of the responsibilities of the feeder coach is to start preparing players and their parents for the day when they will not be playing as much or may even get cut. If parents of young athletes can learn to not hang their own self-image on their child's level of athletic success, it can have a positive impact on the healthy growth of their child.

- *Counsel athletes who have matured early and those who are going to mature late* about how their roles will potentially change. Early maturers and their parents need to understand that a fully developed 6-foot seventh grader is probably going to have a different (and often a diminished) role as a 6-foot senior, and it is not something in their control. Smart players will learn to look ahead and adjust their games to allow them to continue to be an important part of the team. In this regard, for example, they may learn to see the enormous value to a team of their becoming a role player. Players who are caught by surprise about how their maturity or physical level affects their playing time going forward may lose their love of the game if they are not always an "all-star" or even blame the coach for a lower level of success than they enjoyed when they were younger. These are not easy conversations, but they can really help the athlete, the parents, and the coach at the next level. Late-maturing players need to be encouraged to stay with the game and continue working, while their bodies catch up with their heart. Their best athletic days are ahead of them, and their roles on most teams will likely expand.

- *Provide opportunities for interaction* between the high school coach and your players. It may be as simple as sending a schedule of games and practices to the coach or players at the next level, or providing the high school coach with an opportunity to help coach part of one of your practices. Often, just meeting and speaking with the high school coach will give the younger athletes confidence and help ease their transition.

- *Speak supportively* to parents and players about the high school coach, program, team, and school. Nothing can destroy a program faster than to have disloyalty within the coaching ranks.

As the feeder coach, you can be a big part of the success of the high school program, and place the needs of kids first by sending the high school coaches young athletes who have *a positive athletic attitude, can focus for two hours, practice hard, take correction as a compliment, and can put the team ahead of themselves.*

CHAPTER 12

The Role of Parents in Athletics

Part of the successful experience for the athlete involves the communication triangle between the parent, athlete, and coach. This chapter focuses on the parent's role, but the summary addresses suggestions for all three groups.

The involvement of parents in the athletic experience of their children is a given. Without question, all parents should be part of this area of growth in their children. Their involvement affects their own child, the coach, the rest of the team, the other parents, and the officials. How they choose to be involved is a choice they have. This chapter focuses on the parent's role from the perspective of the athlete. In the more than three decades that I was a coach, I frequently asked the players on my teams a series of questions about the role of adults in their experience. In the process, I learned many things that helped me as a coach. I also learned many things that young people would like to tell their parents but probably never will.

One of the questions I am asked frequently by coaches is, "how much did kids change over the course of your coaching career?" My response is always the same, "the athletes changed very little, but the parents changed dramatically." While some current parental reactions can undoubtedly be traced to either the professional model of sport or the media, most problems with parents and sport are self-generated. Too many households place an overemphasis on sports at the expense of sportsmanship and support. As a result, the number of parents who cross the appropriate line of support or encouragement to intolerable interference has increased. In a similar display of misplaced priorities, too many parents seem to be more concerned with attracting the attention of college scouts, than just enjoying their child's high school years and letting their child's advancement to college take its own path.

With athletes focusing on a single sport year-round (many at a very early age), the pressure for success in that sport mounts. Parents are making large financial investments in private tutors and conditioning coaches, and doing whatever is necessary to give their kids the opportunity to participate on "select" out-of-season teams to ensure that their kids get as much of an advantage as possible.

As the focus has shifted from playing for the school team to being part of an all-star team outside of school, parents have become more and more involved. Even within the school setting, athletes routinely transfer to another school to play with better players or to be a part of a specific program where they will be more easily "seen." With loyalty only for their own child, these shortsighted adults have been one of the main causes of coaching turnover and burnout.

When I have the opportunity to speak at school parents' meetings, I am not there to represent the coaches or the administrators, but rather the athletes. In most instances involving the sports arena, adults are facilitators, at best, and, at worst, trespassers. My efforts to speak at these meetings have taught me a great deal about my role as a coach and a father. For example, I have learned there are some special things adults can do to help young people enjoy their athletic experience and help them through this age. I also learned that athletes want adults to be part of the inherently fun aspects of sport.

Even today, most parents mean well, but may not be aware of how they can meaningfully help the athletes reach their goals and improve performance. If handled correctly, with both parent and coach working together for the benefit of the athlete, the athletic experience can provide a very positive, developmental encounter for the participants. In order to ensure that the athletic experience is, indeed, positive, everyone in the process (coaches and parents alike) must always remember that the kids' needs must come first.

As a rule, when parents start a young child out athletically, it is considered to be a "joint venture." The general feeling among most parents is that they are sharing their child's athletic experience with him. In turn, they have a requirement to be involved. In the process athletics becomes a link with their children…an enhanced level of communication…something that is shared. Another factor that impacts on the situation is the fact that, when children are under the age of 10, their main goal is usually to please their parents. The parent is always a credible source of knowledge. Everything the parents say is right, a scenario that most parents like. To the dismay (and shock) of many parents, a number of things change as the athlete enters adolescence. As such, learning when and how to diminish the parent's involvement becomes an issue for both parties.

As kids grow older and more independent, parents need to realize that they should stay close to their children, but focus on their kids' needs. Especially in athletics, this is a time for kids. Parents and coaches constantly send powerful messages to athletes, and those messages should not conflict. Since 70% of all young people are done competing in a team sport activity by the age of 12, it becomes even more important that a child's parents, as early as possible, do what they can to facilitate his growth, help his performance, and keep their own proper perspective.

With regard to the role of parents in athletics, the following are some of the things that I learned from having my athletes write answers to questions I posed to them. In over 30 years of coaching, I asked questions of my athletes and heard the same responses, regardless of age, gender, or sport. These suggestions reflect the athlete's point of view. The issues covered focus on three important times – before, during, and after competition.

Before the First Game

As the season begins, parents are encouraged to ask themselves the following questions:

- Do you want them to play? If so, why?
- What will be a successful season for you as a parent?
- What are your goals for them?
- What do you hope they gain from the experience?
- What do you think their role will be on this team?

After the parents have answered these questions for themselves, they should remember their answers, and then when they have some quiet, uninterrupted time, ask their son or daughter the following questions. When their child responds, the parents should just listen without talking.

- Why are you playing?
- What is a successful season?
- What goals do you have?
- What do you think your role will be on the team?

Once the parents have heard their kids' answers and compared them to their own responses, if both sets of expectations are the same, great. On the other hand, if the parents' responses are different from their children's, the kids need their parents to change their attitudes and accept theirs. No questions.

When differences occur, and the parent does not drop his expectations, trouble can begin for the athlete. For example, if the reason a person's son or daughter gives for playing is like most young people, it will usually have something to do with "fun, joy, loving the game." On the other hand, if the parent's goals are something other than that, a conflict eventually will arise. If the parent's reasons for why the child is participating in athletics involves the perception that the young athlete will eventually "get a college scholarship," two completely different sets of expectations exist. The resultant pressure that will undoubtedly arise will not help the player's performance or make the season enjoyable for anyone involved (player, parent, or coach).

Many athletes consistently relate their feelings that their parents do not understand their roles, and almost always feel that their role is larger than what the athlete knows it to be. This situation often turns into frustration and second-guessing, and frequently puts the athlete in the middle between coach and parent, in a position where the athlete can only lose.

Only one guarantee exists during a normal athletic season – it will not be "perfect." Even without disagreements between parents, players, and coaches, problems will always occur with relationships, playing time, and individual and team success. Before these times happen, it is essential that both players and parents have a mutual perspective on everyone's expectations concerning a child's athletic experience.

The next step that needs to be undertaken early in the season is for parents to "release" their son or daughter to the game and to the coach. This recommendation is based on feedback from parents and athletes who have experienced the most athletic success. Parents should always stay close to the situation and get to know their child's coach, especially if their child is young. Parents should fully be aware of who is in their child's life. Once parents are not overly concerned for their child's physical safety, one of the best "gifts" parents can give their children is to release them to the caretakers of their child's sport. As such, during the season, parents must share their child with the coach and the team. The earlier in their child's career they are able to do this, the better it is for their children's development and growth. If a parent feels the need to talk to a coach about a problem, he should call and allow the coach to choose an appropriate time and place. With regard to such problems, some concerns are appropriate, while others are not. Among the concerns that are appropriate for a parent to discuss with his child's coach are:

- Mental and physical treatment of your child
- Ways to help your child improve
- Concerns about your child's behavior

Inappropriate areas of concern that parents should not discuss with their child's coaches include:

- Playing time
- Team strategy or play calling
- Other team members

By releasing their young athlete to the game and coach, parents are telling their children that all successes are theirs, all failures are theirs, and all problems are theirs. There are not many places in a young person's life where their parents can say, "this is your thing." This can't be done with friends, academics, decisions on weekends, or even movies; it can be done in athletics.

The dilemma for most adults is that it is easy for them to see "solutions" in athletic situations and too painful for adults to let their children find their own solutions. On the other hand, it is both necessary and helpful to allow children to work their own way out of troubling dilemmas. Athletics is one of the best places for young people to take risks and to fail. Is there a better place for a kid to take a chance and fail than on the court or field? Understandably, parents do not want their kids to take risks with cars, with drugs, or sexually. On the other hand, no downside exists for allowing a young athlete to take a risk and fail in a game or practice. If young athletes are going to develop into intelligent, instinctive individuals, it is critical that they are given the opportunity to solve their own problems during games. It is more fun for them, and they have an enhanced chance to grow in a meaningful way.

Parents should consider the following "red flags" that indicate that they have not released their young athlete to the game:

- A parent who is continuing to live his own personal athletic dream through his child has not released his child to the game. As a child climbs the competitive ladder of athletics, the parent must consciously separate his dreams from the equation.

- If a parent tends to share in the credit when the child has done well in sport or has been victorious, he is too involved. "I taught her how to shoot that three-pointer" and "I showed him that curveball" are examples of sharing the credit. When asked who does this the most, athletes typically respond that it is their fathers.

- Another red flag is when a parent finds himself trying to solve all of his child's athletic-related problems. ("Let's get everyone together and talk this out" or "I'll just call the coach and solve this.") Young people may laugh and say "that's my mom (or father)." On one hand, it is only natural for a parent to attempt to steer his child through the rough spots in life in order to enhance the child's enjoyment of the athletic experience. But, athletics offers an excellent opportunity to allow kids to learn to solve their own problems. It is alright for parents to teach their child how to talk to teammates or the coach as an authority figure, but they should let their child take responsibility for the actions involved in solving problems.

- If a parent is trying to continue to coach his child when the child probably knows more about the game than the parent does, he has not released the young athlete.

- A parent should realize that he is taking everything too seriously and has not released the child to the activity when:

✓ He is nervous before his child's game.

✓ He has a difficult time bouncing back after his child's team suffers a defeat.

✓ He makes mental notes during a game so he can give his child advice at the conclusion of the game.

✓ He becomes verbally critical of an official.

- Another red flag that is often seen concerning parents with inappropriate expectations occurs when athletes avoid their parents after games or are embarrassed about their parent's involvement. All of these signals indicate that the child's athletic experience is still shared, and the child needs more space.

Parents should understand and accept the fact that all parental assistance involves decisions with a very fine line of judgment.

During the Game

Athletes ask that their parents only do three things during the game. On one hand, the list is not too long. On the other hand, adhering to the list is very hard for many parents because of the emotions involved when their child is "on stage."

In order to help performance (both the athlete's and his teammates), the single most important contribution a parent can make during a game is to model appropriate behavior. What athletes need their parents to model more than anything else is poise and confidence. If parents expect their children to react to the ups and downs involved in a game with poise, then they must model it. It is OK to be excited and encouraging, but if parents want their children to face adversity with self-assurance, then they need to be able to do the same thing. Parents should remember the old maxim: "A child that lives with praise learns to feel good about himself and learns to praise." Children will take their cues from adults (particularly their parents). If an athlete looked at his parents during the game, would he draw confidence, assurance, and poise from what he saw? First of all, the athlete should not be looking at his parents during a game, he should be focusing on playing. If he is looking to his parents either for approval or out of fear, it is another red flag that the parents are too involved and have not released their child to the game.

The second responsibility athletes state that they need their parents to fulfill during the game is to focus on the team and the team's goals. For the coach, a team is like a family, and the players are all his "kids." By focusing on the team, the adults not only get the attention off of their individual child, but also off all the things that are not in the parent's control (e.g., the score, the referees, the opponents, coaching, and playing conditions). When parents focus on those things beyond their control, it only provides a crutch and helps to build in excuses, which in reality makes the adult a confidence cutter.

The third thing that kids need during the game is to have only one instructional voice offering advice. That voice should be the coach's. If a parent does not believe unwanted advice is a negative factor, he should go to a 10-year-old's soccer game where he does not have emotional involvement and watch and listen as if he were a player on the field.

There are only four roles during a game: spectator, competitor, official, and coach. Everyone involved in athletics would be wise to choose only one of those roles to try to fulfill. If a parent finds himself having difficulty dealing with officiating, he should remember that the officials are there to be in charge of the game, make subjective judgments, enforce the rules, and control play. *Every parent should remember that he does not have the right to interact with a game official.* When a parent criticizes a referee, he is teaching his children that it is OK to challenge authority. Some adults have the false impression that by being in a crowd, they somehow become anonymous. People behaving poorly cannot hide. A ticket to a high school game is not a license to verbally abuse others or be obnoxious.

Every sport requires different skills to play and to be a good encourager. Among the factors that determine the degree of difficulty that a parent may have in acting appropriately when his child engages in a particular sport are the adult's physical distance from the game, and how much subjective judgment is involved by coaches and referees. The closer the parents are in proximity, the more difficult it is to watch and keep everything in perspective. Sitting 50 yards away in the football stands is much easier, for example, than being 20 feet away from home plate in softball.

Judgment is involved in every sport, but not nearly as much in an objective sport, like swimming or track, as in basketball where every referee's whistle could go either way and substitutions by coaches are frequent. Each referee's whistle and every coach's substitution can be questioned by anyone in attendance, thereby making it more difficult for an adult with emotional ties to the contest to remain poised and encouraging. Almost all parents believe that their child should play more or have a bigger role on the team. As such, it is very difficult for parents to be objective. Coaches, on the other hand, can be objective.

Another factor that makes a parent's task even more difficult (to a point) is the soloist or spotlight elements of some sports. Gymnastics and wrestling are sports where the spectators are close to the action. In sports such as these lots of subjective judgment exists. Because the athletes are in a spotlight, some very difficult times are created for the parents. As the adults, parents need to learn to watch whatever sport their children have chosen to play and provide what they need most.

On one hand, if parents are able to act appropriately, players indicate that they love to have them present at their games. On the other hand, if the parents cannot adhere to reasonable standards of behavior concerning modeling, poise, and confidence, many athletes state that all factors considered, they would rather have their parents stay home.

After the Game

In my coaching career, I always tried to ask my athletes a series of questions when they were leaving my program. For example, they were asked to look back over all the years they played and identify the most enjoyable part of the whole experience (best memory), and the least favorable part of the whole experience (worst memory). For adults, the hardest time of their child's athletic experience often occurs during the game. For athletes, however, games represent reward (practice is over, and they get to play). When it comes to recalling their least-enjoyable memory, many athletes will name "after the game" and often specifically "after the game in the car with my parents." This situation is often when the most confidence cutting, confrontation, and confusion occurs for the athlete. Unfortunately, some high school athletes do not want to go home after the game because they do not want to face the questioning or criticism. What they need most at these times is not another coach, but a parent (i.e., "just be my Dad").

Fortunately, such a situation does not defy a meaningful solution. As such, in order to help establish a more wholesome atmosphere after the game, most athletes desperately want their parents to give them *time and space* at the end of a game.

All parents hope that their children can grow up to have healthy relationships. Athletics is one of the best places in a young person's life to practice relationship-building. Given the nature of sports, athletes must rely on relationships to succeed in team sports. They need to have confident, meaningful relationships with their teammates and coaches. Yet in the car after the game, a single comment like, "Why does Sally get all the shots?" may mean to the adult, "I think you are a good shooter too," but is interpreted by the athlete to be, "Sally is a ball hog." Questioning remarks like, "Why does coach play a zone?"; "Why don't you guys throw the ball deep instead of running on first down?"; or "Why does the coach have your first baseman playing so close?" can unintentionally undermine the coach's authority.

While the aforementioned questions may be intended by a parent to show his son or daughter that he is an ally or shares interest in the sport, they are often interpreted by that athlete as the parent saying, "In my opinion, your coach doesn't know what he is doing." Athletes do not need adults to question their actions, the actions of other players, or the coach's decisions concerning strategy or playing time. Parents should ask themselves if they can be a source of confidence and help build relationships on the team under the following conditions:

- When their child played well, but the team lost

- When their child played poorly

- When their child played very little or did not play at all

In these scenarios, particularly, parents should give their children the space and time they need to recover. The more competitive the athlete and the more competitive the sport, the more time and space players need. Parents should leave their children alone until they are receptive to interaction with them, and then when they do come to them, parents should give them quiet understanding, be a reflective listener, and bring them back to their bigger perspective. Uninvited conversations that occur after the game are often resented by the athlete. Instead of bringing the parent and athlete closer, players often clam up and send the message, "I don't want to talk about it now." Parents should keep their corrections and criticisms in check and let their child bring the game to them if they want. Good athletes learn better when they seek their own answers. The only time parents should initiate the conversation in this situation is when their children may have exhibited a behavior in the game that would not be acceptable at home (e.g., profanity, disrespect of authority, etc.). Even then, parents should choose their comments and timing carefully, being aware of the emotions of the moment. When confronting a behavior that would not be acceptable in their home, parents should discuss it as a parent to a child, not a parent to an athlete. One comment from a parent that can always be sincerely said and received by a young athlete is, "I love watching you play."

Many young athletes often indicate that conversations with their parents after a game have somehow made them feel as if their value as a person was somehow tied to playing time or winning or losing athletic contests. Almost without exception, it is unlikely that the parents of those kids had any intention of giving that impression. Yet in a simple conversation following a game, a parent can send that exact message. When asked what was said or done to make the athlete feel that way, many players indicated that their parents' responses were often as simple as, "my dad always seems happier when we win," or "my parents are always a lot more quiet when I don't play much," or "when we lose, my dad tells me all the things I did wrong." In reality, these are just the athlete's perceptions of the words or actions of a probably well-meaning adult who may actually have been trying to support or connect with his child, but just wasn't sure how to do it.

Summary Points

❑ *Player's role:*

- Play the game for fun

- Be gracious when you win and graceful when you lose

- Respect and abide by the rules of the game
- Put the team ahead of yourself in every situation
- Accept decisions made by those in authority
- Demonstrate respect for your opponents, coaches, and teammates
- Be accountable for your own actions
- Develop a teachable spirit that allows you to take correction as a compliment
- Accept and embrace the discipline involved in athletics, because it benefits the team
- Develop a feeling of pride based upon "shared joy" of the team, and do not have pride that emanates from arrogance or a sense of entitlement
- Be an athlete of character

❑ *Coach's role:*

- Coach for the love of the game and the love of the athlete
- Put the welfare of your athletes above winning
- Abide by the judgment of the officials and accept the rules of the game as "mutual agreements" required to play within the spirit of the game
- Reward effort and behavior and not outcome
- Give dignity to mistakes made with full speed and attention
- Lead with character and by example
- Put the needs of the team ahead of any individual
- Constantly work to improve your knowledge and ability to teach the game and the athletes
- Be willing to confront incorrect behavior or less than an all-out effort
- Encourage multiple-sport participation
- Keep the game simple and fun
- Be willing to work with parents for the benefit of the individual athlete
- Develop a positive-demanding coaching style

❑ *Parent's role:*

- Attend as many games as possible
- Be a model, not a critic; model appropriate behavior, poise, and confidence

- Attend preseason team meetings
- Do everything possible to make the athletic experience positive for your child and others
- View the game with team goals in mind
- Attempt to relieve competitive pressure, not increase it
- Encourage multiple-sport participation
- Release your children to the coach and the team
- Look upon opponents as friends involved in the same experience
- Accept the judgment of the officials and coaches; remain in control
- Accept the results of each game; do not make excuses
- Demonstrate winning and losing with dignity
- Dignify mistakes made by athletes who are giving their best effort and concentration
- Be an encourager – encourage athletes to keep their perspective in both victory and defeat
- Be a good listener
- Accept the goals, roles, and achievements of your child

All adults involved in sport need to do their part and provide the athlete with the help and assistance he really needs to perform well. As such, parents need to address the following critical issues:

- Ask their children questions about why they play, what their goals and roles are, and then accept young athletes' reasons as their own.
- Once parents know their children are safe physically and emotionally, they should release them to the experience (the game, the team, and the coach).
- During the game, parents should model poise and confidence and keep their focus on the team.
- After the game, parents should give their children space and time, and leave them alone.
- Parents should be confidence builders by maintaining a consistent perspective and not saying or doing anything that will have their children feel like their self-worth is somehow tied to playing time or outcome of a game.

When parents stop and analyze the athletic experience for their children, the reasons they want their kids to play sports involve providing an opportunity to develop physically and emotionally and to enjoy themselves. The side benefit of playing sports is that kids are given a good opportunity to learn how to work and get along with others, to take good risks in a public arena and survive, to learn to set and achieve goals by developing positive work habits, to learn how to succeed and fail with dignity, and to develop friendships outside the family unit that can last for a lifetime.

Relatively speaking, being an athlete in school lasts a short time. Kids want their parents to be part of their positive athletic memories. Parents need to be the individuals who see the big picture and bring their children back to reality when necessary. If young people are making good decisions about drugs, friends, and academics, then sports are just dessert. On the other hand, if a child is not making good decisions about those kinds of things, no amount of athletic success by a young athlete will justify allowing a parent to overlook his child's other choices.

EPILOGUE

Coaching offers an exceptional opportunity to have a positive effect on the lives of others. In this regard, perhaps no legacy of the coaching profession is more important than developing character in young people. Such a legacy will not occur without commitment and caring. It will require that you make good choices. It will demand that you follow a path of principled convictions.

The renowned Penn State football coach, Joe Paterno, once recalled a speech that he had heard at a University function. This speech titled, *Anyway*, provides a basic framework for those coaches who care enough about their profession to give it their best:

Anyway
People are unreasonable, illogical, and self-centered.
Love Them Anyway
If you do good, people will accuse you of selfish, ulterior motives.
Do Good Anyway
If you are successful, you will not fault friends and true enemies.
Succeed Anyway
The deed you do today will be forgotten tomorrow.
Do Good Anyway
Honesty and frankness make us very vulnerable.
Be Honest and Frank Anyway
People favor underdogs but follow only top dogs.
Fight for Some Underdogs Anyway
What you spend years building may be destroyed overnight.
Build Anyway
People will need help but may attack you when you do help them.
Help People Anyway
Give the world the best of all and you still may get mistreated.
Give the World the Best You Can Anyway
Always give it the best that you have, *Anyway*.

Coaching – The Profession of Eternal Value

A legacy is different than an inheritance. An inheritance is something that is given to you. You may or may not know the history, meaning or how it was developed. A legacy is when part of your life or beliefs is relived in the lives of others. Although it may not be your primary focus or intention, coaching provides an opportunity for creating a legacy in the lives of your athletes.

Athletes recall what it means to have someone whom they call "Coach" in their life. As such, a coach is someone who:

- Made me one of the lucky ones – fortunate enough to have had someone special in my life
- Believed in me, someone who had confidence in my talents and ability, but also in my character and significance
- Was able to see more in me and not less, and because he saw more, he expected more
- Inspired my trust; therefore, I trusted my training – my coach was instantly believable
- Really knew me
- Was someone I could always call on for help, encouragement, and counsel
- Kept me grounded in the important things
- Was someone whose value structure and approach to life enabled me to be better able to raise my own children
- Inspired me to expect more from myself that I ever dreamed was possible
- Taught me that winning is not as important as giving your best; my coach still inspires my best
- Gave me pause every time I work hard or have a difficult task to think back to him
- Gave me an inner voice
- Gave me a base of character – work habits, a team-first attitude
- Taught me how to interact with family and colleagues
- Taught me to deny my own selfish ambitions for the benefit of my "teammates"
- Made me want to coach – teach
- Made me a better parent and spouse
- Taught me that if I win by compromising my integrity or character, I haven't won at all

- Helped me learn to celebrate effort, get over mistakes, and focus on things I can control
- Allowed me to compete fearlessly
- Built my framework of confidence, and self esteem
- Provided me with a positive guide – a positive voice
- Enabled me to have a broad-based, values-oriented perspective in all areas of life
- Gave me lessons in life with which would live with forever, including the fact that playing ball was just a by-product of what he was teaching to me
- Served as my "life time coach," taught me life-time skills – provided the clarity and perspective early in my life, that I sought later in life
- Taught me to never waiver from my personal beliefs; reinforced my need to stay the course
- Made me feel comfortable and safe with sharing my heart
- Got past the personal clutter; spoke directly and honestly; just said "here it is"
- Was a person to whom I will never be able to return the favors he has bestowed on me
- Didn't seek appreciation; had a "serves-first" approach
- Gave me the confidence to overcome challenges
- Made me a reflection of his personality and passion
- Was there for me in tough times – there for me in great times
- Provided feeling of confidence, meaning, and direction to me
- Taught me the skills necessary to be successful in all of life
- Gave me a foundation that provided the driving force for all future success that I might have
- Taught me how to believe in and rely on teammates
- Modeled a philosophy of sport that turned into a philosophy of life for me
- Became a large part of my life and of who I am
- Served as my mentor for life
- Was a person to whom I go to always seek counsel and advice, no matter what the circumstances
- Was my other parent
- Was an individual whom I loved and continue to love
- Taught me through his actions and words that coaching is the profession of eternal value

ABOUT THE AUTHOR

Bruce Eamon Brown is a special presenter for the NAIA's "Champions of Character Program." Previously, he served as the athletic director at Northwest College in Kirkland, Washington. A retired coach, he worked at every level of education in his more than three decades of teaching and coaching. His coaching experiences included basketball, football, volleyball, and baseball at the junior high and high school levels, and basketball at the junior college and college levels. He was involved with championship teams at each level of competition.

Brown is a much sought-after speaker, who frequently addresses coaches, players, and parents on selected aspects concerning participation in sport. He has written several books, including the highly acclaimed *1001 Motivational Messages and Quotes: Teaching Character Through Sport*. He has also been the featured speaker on several well-received instructional videos:

- *Basketball Skills and Drills for Younger Players:*

    Volume 7 – Individual Defense

    Volume 8 – Team Defense

    Volume 9 – Fast Break

    Volume 10 – Zone Offense

    Volume 11 – The Role of Parents in Athletics

- *Fun Ways to End Basketball Practice*
- *Team Building Through Positive Conditioning*
- *Redefining the Term "Athlete"—Using the Five Core Values*
- *How to Teach Character Through Sport*

Brown and his wife, Dana, have five daughters, Allison, Katie, Shannon, Bridget, and Dana. The family resides in Camano Island, Washington.

Additional Resources from Bruce Brown and Coaches Choice

- **1001 Motivational Messages and Quotes**
  2001 • 198 pages • 1-58518-377-6 • $19.95

- **How to Teach Character Through Sport**
  2003 • 58 minutes • 827008734832 • $40.00

- **Redefining the Term "Athlete"—Using the Five Core Values**
  2003 • 31 minutes • 827008733033 • $40.00

- **The Role of Parents in Athletics**
  2002 • 46 minutes • 827008641437 • $40.00

- **Team Building Through Positive Conditioning**
  2002 • 62 minutes • 827008661930 • $40.00

To Place Your Order:

Toll Free: 888-229-5745
Mail: Coaches Choice
            P.O. Box 1828, Monterey, CA 93942
FAX: 831-372-6075
ONLINE: www.coacheschoice.com